"Learning a language, modern or
our human language acquisition abilities. For too long ancient languages
more like math than languages. The focus was on paradigms and piecemeal analysis.
Tools like Scheumanns' *According to Their Kinds* allow us to break free from the worn
out grammar-translation models and engage students with stimuli rooted in research on
how we acquire languages. This well-designed visual resource recognizes that memory
utilizes sense-based cues to acquire vocabulary. I am sure that *According to Their Kinds*
will serve teachers and students extremely well, resulting in deeper comprehension and
longer retention of Biblical Hebrew."

> **Robert D. Holmstedt**, Professor of Biblical Hebrew and Ancient West Semitic
> Languages, University of Toronto; co-author, *Beginning Biblical Hebrew: A
> Grammar and Illustrated Reader*

"*According to Their Kinds* is a splendid resource for moving Hebrew learners away from
thinking about vocabulary as merely English glosses toward broader cognitive concepts.
The integration of words, clauses, and images serves to reinforce better understanding of
Hebrew language. Furthermore, the chapter groupings are ideal for conceptualizing the
relationships between similar terms and ideas. This tool will help beginning, intermediate,
and even advanced students find renewed enjoyment in studying Hebrew vocabulary."

> **Chip Hardy**, Associate Professor of Old Testament & Semitic Languages,
> Southeastern Baptist Theological Seminary; author, *Exegetical Gems from Biblical
> Hebrew*

"If we're not careful, with resources like Picture Hebrew and *According to Their Kinds*,
learning Hebrew vocabulary might actually become intuitive and enjoyable. We, biblical
Hebrew teachers, won't stand for that! For those teachers of the language who, however,
want their students to learn more and suffer less, I highly recommend this resource."

> **Jeremiah J. Davidson**, Rector and Hebrew Professor, The Pastors School at First
> Baptist Church of Atibaia, Brazil

"Learning Hebrew through traditional Hebrew-word-to-English-word vocabulary cards
is monotonous, time-consuming work that leaves students translating into English rather
than reading Hebrew. *According to Their Kinds*, a topically organized visual dictionary
of Biblical Hebrew, helps students to think in Hebrew (and expedites the vocabulary
acquisition process) by giving students a picture to associate the meaning directly with
the Hebrew word, rather than using English as a gateway. A Biblical text is provided to
clarify the meaning and give an additional anchor for the memory. Hebrew students and
teachers who use this resource will give thanks for the Scheumanns' labors!"

> **John C. Beckman**, Associate Professor of Old Testament, Bethlehem College &
> Seminary; author, *Williams' Hebrew Syntax* 3rd ed. (Revised and Expanded)

"Mastering the vocabulary of the Hebrew Bible has always been a problem for students. Picture Hebrew is an important advance in the teaching of the vocabulary of the Hebrew Bible and is distinguished from previous attempts by combining visual and conceptual aspects of lexical items. By grouping words into conceptual categories, students make connections between semantically related words in ways that stimulate the learning and retention of vocabulary items. The beautiful pictures allow students to experience the realia of ancient Israel. In this way, students are able to glimpse the alterity of the world and the world-view of the biblical text. As a companion to the electronic app of Picture Hebrew, *According to their Kinds* provides students in our digital media culture a relevant and effective means to acquire the vocabulary of the Hebrew Bible."

> **Jacobus A. Naudé and Cynthia L. Miller-Naudé**, Senior Professors, Department of Hebrew, University of the Free State, South Africa

"The more senses we can engage in the study of the biblical languages the better! I hope students will be helped to learn Hebrew vocabulary by this creative and visually engaging resource."

> **James M. Hamilton**, Professor of Biblical Theology, The Southern Baptist Theological Seminary

"Thank you to Picture Hebrew for another useful resource, this one for reviewing the most common vocabulary items in the Hebrew Bible in a way that does not use English glosses as the primary interface, and grouping them into categories for easier recall. The use of pictures allows the learning to remain in Hebrew, so key for effective internalizing of the language."

> **Brian Schultz**, Associate Professor of Biblical & Theological Studies, Fresno Pacific University

"This is a brilliant tool for acquiring and for reviewing Hebrew vocabulary—concise, well-organized, and visually engaging. I would highly recommend it for self-study as well as for use in any style of Hebrew classroom."

> **Sarah Lynn Baker**, Lecturer in Hebrew Language and Literature, The University of Texas at Austin

"Scheumann and Scheumann's *According to Their Kinds* is an accessible and well thought-out pedagogical tool. Instead of boring word-lists, students are presented with clear and beautiful images that illustrate vocabulary—engaging different parts of the brain and encouraging natural language learning. *According to Their Kinds* will be an indispensable resource for first-year Hebrew students."

> **John Screnock**, Research Fellow in Hebrew Bible, Faculty of Oriental Studies at University of Oxford

"We naturally acquire language coincidentally and contextually, first by hearing sounds and then associating those sounds with meaning in context we see and experience. More formally, parents may use a "wordbook" with their infant where a word or phrase is attached to a picture. When parents read to their small children, those books are full of illustrations that help them associate what they are hearing with concepts. In the quest of acquiring a reading ability in Biblical Hebrew the Scheumanns have provided a resource so much more effective than flashcards with a Hebrew word on one side and an English gloss on the other. They offer a tool that associates words with an icon to aid in visualizing the concept as well as with an example of its use in context. *According to Their Kinds* is a gift to anyone wishing to learn to read and study Jesus' Bible."

Paul Ferris, Professor of Hebrew Bible Emeritus, Bethel Seminary.

"I dreamed of creating a resource like this for many years; the Scheumanns have made my dream a reality. With gripping images, biblical-contextual examples, and helpful thematic categorizations, this tool is for everyone who desires to truly internalize Biblical Hebrew vocabulary. I eagerly await a second volume!"

Marcus A. Leman, PhD. Old Testament, The Southern Baptist Theological Seminary

"*According to Their Kinds* is optimized to help you log information into long-term memory. A number of associative strategies are employed for this purpose. In particular, this Biblical Hebrew dictionary is unique in providing illustrations for nearly every entry. Additionally, many of those illustrations are based on recognizable Bible passages and characters, each one accompanied by a sentence based on actual biblical text. Finally, the grouping of words according to semantic domains, and often in synonym/antonym pairs, helps cement the meaning of words in relation to others in the language system. I highly recommend this dictionary as a learning tool for all students of Biblical Hebrew. Even those who have already learned much Hebrew vocabulary by other means will be able to see and remember Hebrew words in a new way."

Jacques E. J. Boulet, PhD. Biblical Hebrew Grammar and Linguistics, University of Toronto

"*According to Their Kinds* is a fantastic resource that brings Biblical Hebrew vocabulary to life in a new way. Recommended for students who want to expand their vocabulary and strengthen the direct link between a concept and its Hebrew word without dependence on English as a medium. Clear contextualized illustrations and example sentences from the biblical text make this a great learning tool for really internalizing the language instead of memorizing lists of words."

Bethany Case, Linguist Missionary, Equatorial Guinea

According to Their Kinds

A Biblical Hebrew Picture Dictionary

Jesse R. Scheumann
Merissa Scheumann

Picture Hebrew

According to Their Kinds: A Biblical Hebrew Picture Dictionary

Copyright © 2019 by Jesse R. Scheumann and Merissa Scheumann

Illustration copyright © 2019 by Merissa Scheumann

Published by Picture Hebrew

Cover design: Brian Fergus

Cover images: Merissa Scheumann

First printing 2019

Printed in the United States of America

ISBN: 978-1086429718

www.picturehebrew.com

To our former Hebrew students,
and many more to come,
we have toiled joyfully with you in mind.

ACKNOWLEDGMENTS

This book is the culmination of five years of work. It began with frantic sketches on 3" x 5" cards traced in marker before our first child arrived in April 2014. We had exhausted the available Hebrew picture resources at the time, and we wanted something for the most frequent vocabulary. We showed those (now) embarrassing illustrations to our classmates at a Hebrew ulpan that summer, and surprisingly some expressed interest in getting a set of cards for themselves. We then launched the first of three different renditions of the flashcards to bring them to the public in 2017. Even the third rendition has been through three separate editions, as we have revised all of the drawings based on user feedback.

Our best feedback has come from our own students. We would like to thank the TBI classes of 2014–2017, the PH class of 2017–2018, and the Sattler College class of 2018–2019. Our Plumfund supporters in 2017 enabled us to make high-quality digital scans of the third rendition of the drawings. Our Kickstarter backers in 2018 empowered us to launch an app to reach a larger audience and receive even more feedback. And our parents have supported us every step of the way. Thank you!

Cody Hinkle was the first one (we took seriously) to suggest that we combine the pictures into a book. He gave very valuable constructive criticism at the conceptual stage and at later stages of the book creation, as did Brian Schultz, Benjamin Kantor, Marcus Leman, Sarah Baker, Cam Hamm, Caleb Smoker, and Bethany Case. As Hebrew teachers, they flagged a number of errors for us, and they helped us mold the book into a more pedagogically-sound language resource.

Many other Hebrew scholars gave generously of their time to review a mostly-finalized book draft. To those who endorsed this book, we are deeply grateful. Several gave us comments for improvement. We thank Jacobus Naudé, Cynthia Miller-Naudé, Robert Holmstedt, Kevin Chau, John Beckman, Bernard Levinson, Lee Fields, Jacques Boulet, and John Screnock. Once again, the design, style, and layout of the book, and even some drawings, improved from their remarks. While we acknowledge all of these people in these last two paragraphs for their positive impact, let the reader understand that if any lack remains in this book, the regrettable blame rests solely at our feet.

We would also like to thank some of our former students who gave critical feedback this summer on how intuitive the latest editions of the drawings are, as well as the page layouts in this dictionary. These include Lois Friesen, Blair Johnson, Timothy Miller, Christina Boyum, Meredith Nyberg, Annemarie Metcalf, and Tyler Foster. Thank you!

Finally, it is no perfunctory act to acknowledge God, since "in him we live and move and have our being" (Acts 17:28). Our sincere prayer is, "Not to us, O LORD, not to us, but to your name give glory, for the sake of your steadfast love and faithfulness" (Ps 115:1).

CONTENTS

ABBREVIATIONS

ADJ	=	adjective (modifies a noun)
ADV	=	adverb (modifies a verb)
c	=	common (gender)
f	=	feminine (gender)
HI	=	Hif'il (a verbal stem, often for causing an action)
HSTFL	=	Hishtafel (a verbal stem with only one root: חוה)
HTP	=	Hitpa'el (a verbal stem, often reflexive)
imp	=	imperative (conjugation for giving commands)
inf	=	infinitive (a verbal noun that does not inflect)
m	=	masculine (gender)
N	=	noun
NI	=	Nif'al (a verbal stem, often passive)
p	=	plural
PI	=	Pi'el (a verbal stem, often for causing a state)
PREP	=	preposition
Q	=	Qal (the default verbal stem, sometimes called Pa'al)
s	=	singular
vyqtl	=	vayyiqtol (conjugation for narrative past tense)
1	=	first person ("I, we")
2	=	second person ("you")
3	=	third person ("he," "she," "they")

או	=	אוֹ	=	"or"
כג	=	כִּנּוּי גוּף	=	"pronoun"
ו	=	וְ	=	"and"
פ	=	פּוֹעַל	=	"verb"
שע	=	שֵׁם עֶצֶם	=	"noun"
שת	=	שֵׁם תּוֹאַר	=	"adjective"
תפ	=	תּוֹאַר פּוֹעַל	=	"adverb"

TRANSLITERATION

The transliteration we use is non-technical and is meant to be intuitive to a broad audience. We present the major Hebrew dialect spoken today in Israel.[1] While we believe it is the dominant approach, it is by no means a universal practice for reading Biblical Hebrew. Professors with another preference should provide their own pronunciation guide.

Alef	א	' (glottal stop) as in uh'oh[2]	*Lamed*	ל	l as in lake
Bet	ב	**b** as in **b**oy	*Mem*	מ\ם	**m** as in **m**an
Vet	ב	**v** as in **v**ase	*Nun*	נ\ן	**n** as in **n**oon
Gimel	ג\ג	**g** as in **g**oat	*Samex*	ס	**s** as in **s**eed
Dalet	ד\ד	**d** as in **d**og	*Ayin*	ע	' as in uh'oh
He	ה	**h** as in **h**at	*Pe*	פ	**p** as in **p**ie
Vav	ו	**v** as in **v**ase	*Fe*	פ\ף	**f** as in **f**ish
Zayin	ז	**z** as in **z**oo	*Tsade*	צ\ץ	**ts** as in ca**ts**
Xet	ח	**x** as in Ba**ch**	*Qof*	ק	**q** as in Ira**q**
Tet	ט	**t** as in **t**oy	*Resh*	ר	**r** as in **r**ing
Yod	י	**y** as in **y**ak	*Sin*	שׂ	**s** as in **s**eed
Kaf	כ	**k** as in **k**ey	*Shin*	שׁ	**sh** as in **sh**ed
Xaf	כ\ך	**x** as in Ba**ch**	*Tav*	ת\ת	**t** as in **t**oy

ָ / ֳ	**a** as in f**a**ther	יִ ֵ	**ay** as in **a**y**e**	
ֶ / ֱ	**e** as in b**e**d	ְ	silent/ə as in **e**xcuse	
	i as in mach**i**ne			
ֹ / ֳ	**o** as in sn**o**w	וֹי	**oy** as in s**oy**	
וּ / ֻ	**u** as in fl**u**			

[1] S. Bolozky, "Phonology: Israeli Hebrew," in G. Khan, ed., *Encyclopedia of Hebrew Language and Linguistics*, Vol 3 (Leiden; Boston: Brill, 2013), 113–122. *Alef* and *Ayin* are often unpronounced, in which case they are not transliterated. The vowel letters *Yod* and *He* do not alter vowel sound, so we do not list them in the vowel section.
[2] *Alef* and *Ayin* are only transliterated this way when they begin a word-medial syllable.

PREFACE

Audience and Stages of Use

Acquiring Hebrew vocabulary is often slow and tedious, and yet reading biblical passages is impossible without a large word bank. This dictionary includes all words that occur 100 times or more in the Hebrew Bible, and there are about 50 extra words to round out the vocabulary sections.

According to Their Kinds ushers students into the world of Biblical Hebrew. English is separate and in grayscale at the bottom of the page to keep readers in the target language as much as possible. The vocabulary list is arranged in sections by thematic categories.[1] The pictures proceed from general to specific, as the user scans the page left-to-right and top-to-bottom. There are often correlations between nouns and verbs that are in the same row on facing pages.

We designed this dictionary as an intuitive resource for self-study. It is also an engaging textbook for a beginning or intermediate Hebrew class. I (Jesse) use it in third semester, where I assign a few pages for each class period. Students translate the example sentences for quizzes. In this way, they review the most-important vocabulary from first year, while also adding new vocabulary learned in context of the biblical verses.

An intermediate student can start reading the book cover-to-cover, but a beginner should follow three incremental stages of learning. First, transliteration is included at the bottom of the page to aid in reading and memorizing Hebrew vocabulary. A sideways caret indicates a non-final accent in the Hebrew word.[2] For transliteration, each stressed syllable has

---

[1] The first four main-section headings are taken from J. D. Pleins with J. Homrighausen, *Biblical Hebrew Vocabulary by Conceptual Categories* (Grand Rapids, MI: Zondervan, 2017). We adapted the sub-sections and moved words based on the needs of our list.

[2] We treat words like מַיִם as monosyllabic with a diphthong.

an acute accent mark. There is no audio companion for this book, but it is included for the flashcards, available at picturehebrew.com.

Second, after learning a critical mass of words, a student is able to read the short sentences under the verbs. Third, the sentences for non-verb vocabulary present a more challenging opportunity to read Hebrew.

There are about 50 words that were too abstract to illustrate. These words are in section 5.7 with English translations. This book is primarily a learning tool and secondarily a reference guide. The glossary and index in the back provide easy reference for all Hebrew word entries.

Principles of Illustration

Non-verb illustrations are simple and generic. Verbs illustrate an iconic usage, and each character is recognizable from picture to picture. Most of the illustrations contain a text box in a particular corner to indicate whether the word is a verb (פ), noun (שע), adjective (שת), adverb (תפ), or pronoun (כג). The following principles guided our illustrations:

- The primary figure is centered, foregrounded, and bolded
- All "movement" flows right-to-left
- The illustration captures the central/basic sense of the word
  - Literal sense is preferred over metaphorical sense
  - One meaning is preferred over multiple, unless ...
    - A second meaning is on par with the first as central in the semantic range, or
    - A second meaning is unrelated to the first and would otherwise be confusing even in context
- A word with two meanings has the Hebrew word "or" (או) between the illustrations
- A word with one meaning may be illustrated in bold with a solid line separating it and its antonym or a previous scene (given for context)
- Two antonyms with one form each are illustrated on the same card and separated by the Hebrew word "and" (ו)
- If a general word could be taken as the specific example depicted, an "or ..." (או) in the bottom left corner indicates other possible examples

Explanation of Non-Verb Forms

For every vocabulary entry, we put a backslash between the two Hebrew forms of the same word. We separate two different words (synonyms or antonyms) on the same line with a raised dot.

Noun entries list the singular form and, if attested, the plural form (unless the dual is more common than the plural). The second form shows that many nouns take irregular endings. We list the gender after most nouns. For nouns with mixed data, we list whichever gender is most often reflected. For nouns with no indication, we leave the gender blank.

All adjectives list both the masculine and feminine singular forms. Listing two forms, as with nouns, helps students naturally absorb patterns of inflection, and it enables them to predict the plural forms.

We illustrate only the spatial sense for prepositions, even though most of them have logical extensions. The pictures are designed for beginners who, like children, thrive in absorbing the language as a simple, concrete system. The maturing student who reads biblical texts will pick up on the other uses of these prepositions when they occur in context.

All geographic places that occur over 100 times are included. Each nation's size represents the height of its expansion in a way that does not overlap with another nation.[3] Personal names are not illustrated.

Explanation of Verb Forms

For each verbal entry, we list the 3ms qatal (perfect) and the 3ms yiqtol (imperfect) forms. Under the sentence are four extra forms that are useful to know: infinitive | 2ms imperative | 3ms vayyiqtol | consonantal root.

The rest of this section is technical. Beginning students can skip it. The verb list is derived from roots that occur 100 times or more. Each root is illustrated as Qal if it occurs in that binyan (stem). But many roots are not attested as Qal. In these cases, we illustrate whichever binyan (Nif'al, Pi'el, or Hif'il) occurs most frequently. These words are often best thought of as having approximately the same meaning as Qal.

---

[3] We adapted the maps from T. V. Brisco, *Holman Bible Atlas: A Complete Guide to the Expansive Geography of Biblical History* (Nashville, TN: B&H, 1998).

To teach the binyanim system, we illustrate many derived-binyanim words that have a Qal counterpart. Nif'al often has a passive meaning ("be found" vs. Qal "find"). Pi'el often has a causative-state connotation ("consecrate" vs. Qal "be holy"). Hif'il often has a causative-action sense ("proclaim" vs. Qal "hear"). And Hitpa'el often has a definition reflexive of Qal or Pi'el ("boast" vs. Pi'el "praise"). We do not include Hof'al or Pu'al words. We chose to incorporate a derived-binyan word especially if it occurs 100 times or more, or if its meaning is surprising within the binyanim system.

Explanation of Hebrew Sentences

The sentence in each verb entry is based on the illustrated verse. The verb is converted into a participle. We did this partly to provide another verbal form, but mainly to describe the picture more accurately as a snapshot of an in-progress action. The default word order for participle clauses is subject-predicate.[4] An asterisk marks the sentences that do not employ a participle for semantic or syntactic reasons.

Each sentence in a non-verb entry is a direct quote from the Hebrew Bible. These sentences are harder to read than the verb entries, because they rarely describe the pictures, and because the predicate is unaltered and thus can be in any conjugation. Sometimes we condensed the verse. We also made a couple changes to standardize spelling: all pausal forms are removed, and the 3fs subject pronoun always appears as הִיא. But other variations—like plene vs. defective spelling and an accent shift to avoid stress clash—are maintained from the Masoretic Text.

The translation of all sentences are our own, and the Bible references in parentheses cite the Hebrew versification. An asterisk indicates each instance when the English reference is different.

---

[4] R. Buth, "Word Order in the Verbless Clause: A Generative-Functional Approach," in C. Miller, ed., *The Verbless Clause in Biblical Hebrew* (Winona Lake, IN: Eisenbrauns, 1999), 79–108.

1
The Created Order

1.1
Heavens and Earth

שָׁמַיִם

וַיְכֻלּוּ הַשָּׁמַיִם וְהָאָרֶץ וְכָל־צְבָאָם

שֶׁמֶשׁ

יְהוָה נֹתֵן שֶׁמֶשׁ לְאוֹר יוֹמָם

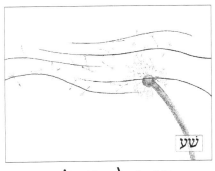

רוּחַ \ רוּחוֹת

וַיּוֹלֶךְ יְהוָה אֶת־הַיָּם בְּרוּחַ קָדִים

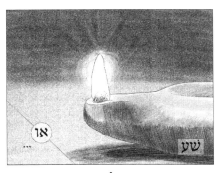

אוֹר

וַיֹּאמֶר אֱלֹהִים יְהִי אוֹר וַיְהִי־אוֹר

---

shamáym
N: heaven, sky (m)
The heavens and the earth and all
their host were finished. (Gen 2:1)

shémesh
N: sun (f)
YHWH gives the sun for light by
day. (Jer 31:35)

rúax / ruxót
N: wind; spirit (f)
YHWH led the sea with an east
wind. (Exod 14:21)

ór
N: light (m)
And God said, "Let there by light,"
and there was light. (Gen 1:3)

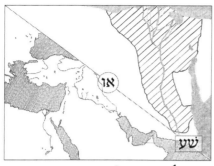

אֶ֫רֶץ \ אֲרָצוֹת

וַתֵּ֫לַהּ אֶ֫רֶץ מִצְרַיִם וְאֶ֫רֶץ כְּנַ֫עַן

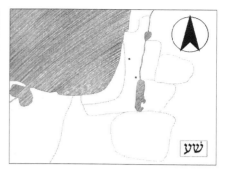

צָפוֹן

כִּי רָעָה אָנֹכִי מֵבִיא מִצָּפוֹן

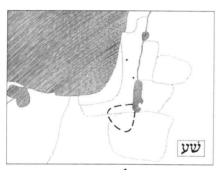

נֶ֫גֶב

וַיִּקַּח יְהוֹשֻׁעַ אֶת־כָּל־הַנֶּ֫גֶב

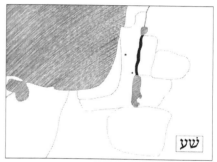

יַרְדֵּן

קוּם עֲבֹר אֶת־הַיַּרְדֵּן הַזֶּה

érets / aratsót
N: land; (known) world, earth (f)
The land of Egypt and the land of
Canaan languished. (Gen 47:13)

négev
N: Negev, arid terrain
And Joshua took all of the Negev.
(Josh 11:16)

tsafón
N: north
"... because I am bringing a disaster
from the north." (Jer 4:6)

yardén
N: Jordan (m)
"Get up, cross this Jordan."
(Josh 1:2)

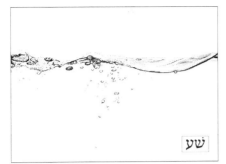

מַיִם

וְהַבּוֹר רֵק אֵין בּוֹ מָיִם

יָם \ יַמִּים

וַיָּבֹאוּ בְנֵי־יִשְׂרָאֵל בְּתוֹךְ הַיָּם

נַ֫חַל \ נְחָלִים

וָאַשְׁלִךְ אֶל־הַנַּ֫חַל הַיֹּרֵד מִן־הָהָר

נָהָר \ נְהָרוֹת

נָהָר יֹצֵא מֵעֵדֶן לְהַשְׁקוֹת אֶת־הַגָּן

---

máym
N: water (m)
And the cistern was empty—there
was no water in it. (Gen 37:24)

náxal / nəxalím
N: stream, wadi (m)
"I threw (it) into the stream that goes
down from the mountain." (Deut 9:21)

yám / yamím
N: sea (m)
And the children of Israel went into
the midst of the sea. (Exod 14:22)

nahár / nəharím
N: river (m)
A river was going out of Eden to
water the garden. (Gen 2:9)

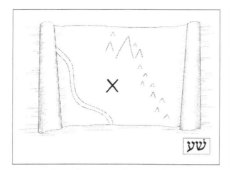

מָקוֹם \ מְקוֹמוֹת

שָׂדֶה \ שָׂדוֹת

וַיִּקְרָא אֶת־שֵׁם־הַמָּקוֹם בֵּית־אֵל

וַיָּבֹא עֵשָׂו מִן־הַשָּׂדֶה וְהוּא עָיֵף

אֲדָמָה \ אֲדָמוֹת

מִגְרָשׁ \ מִגְרָשִׁים

וְקַיִן הָיָה עֹבֵד אֲדָמָה

וּמִגְרְשֵׁיהֶם יִהְיוּ לִבְהֶמְתָּם

---

maqóm / məqomót
N: place, location (m)
And he called the name of the place
"Bethel." (Gen 28:19)

sadé / sadót
N: open field (m)
And Esau came in from the field,
and he was tired. (Gen 25:29)

adamá / adamót
N: ground (f)
And Cain was a worker of ground.
(Gen 4:2)

migrásh / migrashím
N: pastureland (m)
"And their pasturelands shall be for
their livestock." (Num 35:3)

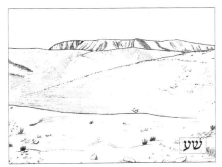

מִדְבָּר

הַר \ הָרִים

וַיְנִעֵם בַּמִּדְבָּר אַרְבָּעִים שָׁנָה

וַיָּבֹא אֶל־הַר הָאֱלֹהִים חֹרֵבָה

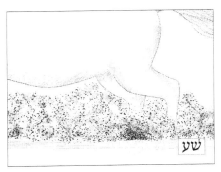

עָפָר

אֵשׁ

וַיִּיצֶר אֱלֹהִים אֶת־הָאָדָם עָפָר

וַתִּפֹּל הָאֵשׁ וַתֹּאכַל אֶת־הָעֹלָה

---

midbár
N: wilderness, desert (m)
"He made them wander in the desert forty years." (Num 32:13)

hár / harím
N: mountain (m)
He came to the mountain of God, to Horeb. (Exod 3:1)

afár
N: dust (m)
And God formed the man out of dust. (Gen 2:7)

ésh
N: fire (f)
And the fire fell and ate the burnt offering. (1 Kgs 18:38)

1.2
Metals and Stone

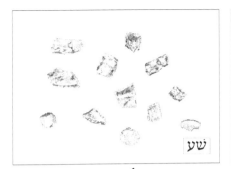

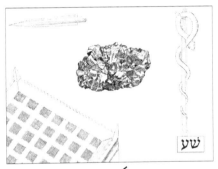

כֶּֽסֶף

הוּשַׁב כַּסְפִּי וְהִנֵּה בְאַמְתַּחְתִּי

זָהָב

וְאַבְרָם כָּבֵד מְאֹד בַּמִּקְנֶה בַּכֶּֽסֶף וּבַזָּהָב

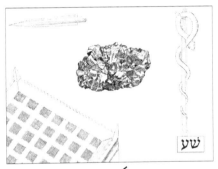

נְחֹֽשֶׁת

וְעָשִׂיתָ כִּיּוֹר נְחֹשֶׁת וְכַנּוֹ נְחֹשֶׁת

אֶֽבֶן \ אֲבָנִים

וַיֶּחֱזַק דָּוִד מִן־הַפְּלִשְׁתִּי בָּאֶֽבֶן

késef N: silver, money (m) "My silver has been returned, and here it is in my sack." (Gen 42:28)	*zaháv* N: gold (m) And Abram was very heavy with silver and with gold. (Gen 13:2)
nəxóshet N: copper, bronze (f) "You shall make a basin out of bronze and its stand of bronze." (Exod 30:18)	*éven / avaním* N: stone, rock (f) David prevailed over the Philistine with the stone. (1 Sam 17:50)

1.3
Plants and Animals

עֵץ \ עֵצִים

וּמֵעֵץ הַדַּעַת טוֹב וָרָע לֹא תֹאכַל

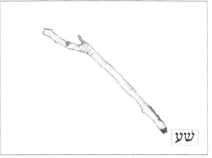

מַקֵּל \ מַקְלוֹת

וַיַּךְ אֶת־הָאָתוֹן בַּמַּקֵּל

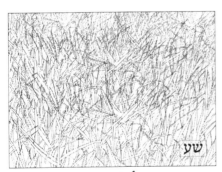

דֶּשֶׁא

בִּנְאוֹת דֶּשֶׁא יַרְבִּיצֵנִי

פֶּרַח \ פְּרָחִים

וַיֹּצֵא מַטֵּה־אַהֲרֹן פֶּרַח

éts / etsím
N: tree, wood (m)
"But from the tree of knowing good and evil you shall not eat." (Gen 2:17)

déshe
N: grass, vegetation (m)
"In pastures of grass he makes me lie down." (Ps 23:2)

maqél / maqlót
N: branch, stick (m)
And he struck the donkey with the stick. (Num 22:27)

pérax / praxím
N: flower, blossom (m)
And the staff of Aaron brought forth a flower. (Num 17:23*)

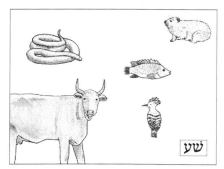

חַיָּה \ חַיּוֹת

כָּל־הַחַיָּה אֲשֶׁר־אִתְּךָ מִכָּל־בָּשָׂר

בְּהֵמָה \ בְּהֵמוֹת

מִן־הַבְּהֵמָה מִן־הַבָּקָר וּמִן־הַצֹּאן

צֹאן

וַיְהִי־הֶבֶל רֹעֵה צֹאן

בָּקָר

וְאֶל־הַבָּקָר רָץ אַבְרָהָם

---

xayá / xayót
N: animal (f)
"Every animal that is with you of all
flesh ..." (Gen 8:17)

bəhemá / bəhemót
N: livestock (f)
"... from the livestock: from the
cattle and from the flock." (Lev 1:2)

tsón
N: flock(s) (m)
And Abel was a shepherd of a flock.
(Gen 4:2)

baqár
N: cattle, herd (m)
And to the cattle Abraham ran.
(Gen 18:7)

כֶּבֶשׂ \ כְּבָשִׂים

וְשָׁחַט אֶת־כֶּבֶשׂ הָאָשָׁם

אַיִל \ אֵילִים

וַיִּשָּׂא אֶת־עֵינָיו וַיַּרְא אַיִל

עֵגֶל \ עֲגָלִים

וָאַשְׁלִכֵהוּ בָאֵשׁ וַיֵּצֵא הָעֵגֶל הַזֶּה

פַּר \ פָּרִים

וְשָׁחַטְתָּ אֶת־הַפָּר לִפְנֵי יְהוָה

kéves / kəvasím
N: young ram, sheep (m)
"He shall slaughter the young ram
of the guilt offering." (Lev 14:25)

áyl / elím
N: ram (m)
He lifted his eyes, and he saw a ram.
(Gen 22:13)

égel / agalím
N: young bull, calf (m)
"I threw it in the fire, and out came
this calf." (Exod 32:24)

pár / parím
N: bull (m)
"And you shall slaughter the bull
before YHWH." (Exod 29:11)

חֲמוֹר \ חֲמוֹרִים

וַתָּקָם וַתִּרְכַּב עַל־הַחֲמוֹר

סוּס \ סוּסִים

וַיָּבֹא נַעֲמָן בְּסוּסוֹ וּבְרִכְבּוֹ

עֵז \ עִזִּים

שַׂעְרֵךְ כְּעֵדֶר הָעִזִּים

גָּמָל \ גְּמַלִּים

פִּנִּיתִי הַבַּיִת וּמָקוֹם לַגְּמַלִּים

---

xamór / xamorím
N: donkey (m)
She arose and rode on the donkey.
(1 Sam 25:42)

sús / susím
N: horse (m)
And Naaman came with his horse
and with his chariot. (2 Kgs 5:9)

éz / izím
N: goat (f)
"Your hair is like the flock of goats."
(Song 4:1)

gamál / gəmalím
N: camel (m)
"I have cleared the house and a place
for the camels." (Gen 24:31)

נָחָשׁ \ נְחָשִׁים

וַיֹּאמֶר הַנָּחָשׁ אֶל־הָאִשָּׁה

אַרְיֵה \ אֲרָיוֹת

וַיִּמְצָאֵהוּ אַרְיֵה בַּדֶּרֶךְ וַיְמִיתֵהוּ

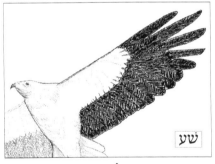

עוֹף

וְהָעוֹף אֹכֵל אֹתָם מִן־הַסַּל

כָּנָף \ כְּנָפַיִם

וָאֶשָּׂא אֶתְכֶם עַל־כַּנְפֵי נְשָׁרִים

---

naxásh / nəxashím
N: snake (m)
And the snake said to the woman.
(Gen 3:4)

óf
N: bird(s) (m)
"And the birds were eating them
from the basket." (Gen 40:17)

aryé / arayót
N: lion (m)
A lion found him in the road and
killed him. (1 Kgs 13:24)

kanáf / kənafáym
N: wing; edge (f)
"And I carried you on wings of
eagles." (Exod 19:4)

1.4
Time and Seasons

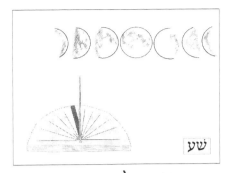

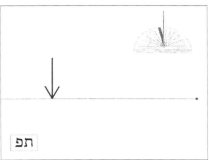

עֵת \ עִתִּים

וַיֹּאמֶר לָהּ בֹּעַז לְעֵת הָאֹכֶל

עַתָּה

עַתָּה יָדַעְתִּי כִּי־גָדוֹל יְהוָה

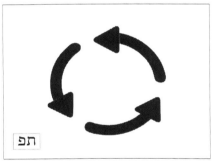

עוֹלָם \ עוֹלָמִים

יְהוָה יִמְלֹךְ לְעֹלָם וָעֶד

תָּמִיד

תֹּאכַל לֶחֶם עַל־שֻׁלְחָנִי תָּמִיד

ét / itím
N: time (f)
And Boaz said to her at the time for
food ... (Ruth 2:14)

olám / olamím
N: forever (m)
"YHWH will reign forever and ever."
(Exod 15:18)

atá
ADV: now
"Now I know that YHWH is great."
(Exod 18:11)

tamíd
ADV/ADJ: regular(ly), always
"You shall eat bread at my table
regularly." (2 Sam 9:7)

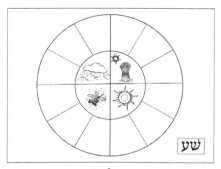

שָׁנָה \ שָׁנִים

אָכְלוּ אֶת־הַמָּן אַרְבָּעִים שָׁנָה

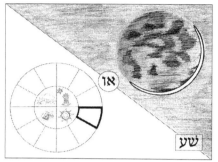

חֹדֶשׁ \ חֳדָשִׁים

וַיֹּאמֶר דָּוִד הִנֵּה־חֹדֶשׁ מָחָר

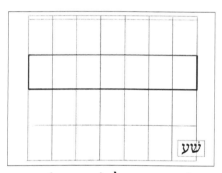

שָׁבוּעַ \ שָׁבֻעוֹת

מַלֵּא שְׁבֻעַ זֹאת וְנִתְּנָה אֶת־זֹאת

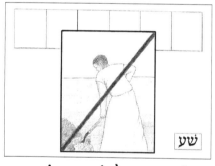

שַׁבָּת \ שַׁבָּתוֹת

וְיוֹם הַשְּׁבִיעִי שַׁבָּת לַיהוָה

---

shaná / shaním
N: year (f)
They ate the manna for forty years.
(Exod 16:35)

xódesh / xodashím
N: new moon; month (m)
And David said, "Behold, tomorrow
is a new moon." (1 Sam 20:5)

shavúa / shavu'ót
N: week (m)
"Complete a week for this one, and
we will give this one." (Gen 29:27)

shabát / shabatót
N: Sabbath, rest (f)
"But the seventh day is a Sabbath to
YHWH." (Exod 20:10)

יוֹם \ יָמִים

וַיִּקְרָא אֱלֹהִים לָאוֹר יוֹם

לַיְלָה \ לֵילוֹת

וְלַחֹשֶׁךְ קָרָא לָיְלָה

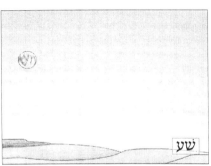

בֹּקֶר \ בְּקָרִים

וַיַּשְׁכֵּם אַבְרָהָם בַּבֹּקֶר

עֶרֶב

וַיְהִי־עֶרֶב וַיְהִי־בֹקֶר יוֹם אֶחָד

---

yóm / yamím
N: day (m)
And God called the light "day."
(Gen 1:5)

láyla / lelót
N: night (m)
And the darkness he called "night."
(Gen 1:5)

bóqer / bəqarím
N: morning (m)
And Abraham rose early in the
morning. (Gen 19:27)

érev
N: evening (m)
There was evening and there was
morning, day one. (Gen 1:5)

2
The Human Order

2.1
Humans and Anatomy

אִישׁ \ אֲנָשִׁים

כֻּלָּנוּ בְּנֵי אִישׁ־אֶחָד

אִשָּׁה \ נָשִׁים

וְדָבַק בְּאִשְׁתּוֹ וְהָיוּ לְבָשָׂר אֶחָד

יֶלֶד \ יְלָדִים

הַיֶּלֶד אֵינֶנּוּ וַאֲנִי אָנָה אֲנִי־בָא

יַלְדָּה \ יְלָדוֹת

קַח־לִי אֶת־הַיַּלְדָּה הַזֹּאת לְאִשָּׁה

ísh / anashím
N: man; husband (m)
"All of us are sons of one man."
(Gen 42:11)

ishá / nashím
N: woman; wife (f)
He shall cling to his wife, and they
shall become one flesh. (Gen 2:24)

yéled / yəladím
N: boy (m)
"The boy, he is no more. And I,
where am I going?" (Gen 37:30)

yaldá / yəladót
N: girl (f)
"Take for me this girl as a wife."
(Gen 34:4)

אָדָם

וַיַּרְא כִּי רַבָּה רָעַת הָאָדָם בָּאָרֶץ

שֵׁם \ שֵׁמוֹת

וַיִּקְרָא הָאָדָם שֵׁם אִשְׁתּוֹ חַוָּה

נַֹעַר \ נְעָרִים

בֶּן־שְׁבַע־עֶשְׂרֵה שָׁנָה וְהוּא נַֹעַר

זָקֵן \ זְקֵנִים

לֵךְ וְאָסַפְתָּ אֶת־זִקְנֵי יִשְׂרָאֵל

---

adám
N: man, humankind; Adam (m)
He saw that great was the evil of
man on the earth. (Gen 6:5)

shém / shemót
N: name (m)
And the man called the name of his
wife "Eve." (Gen 3:20)

ná'ar / nə'arím
N: young man, lad (m)
... seventeen years old, and he was a
young man. (Gen 37:2)

zaqén / zəqením
N: old person, elder (m)
"Go and gather the elders of Israel."
(Exod 3:16)

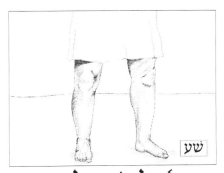

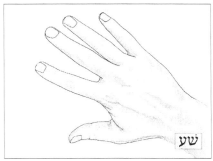

רֶ֫גֶל \ רַגְלַיִם

וְסִֽיסְרָא נָס בְּרַגְלָיו אֶל־אֹ֫הֶל יָעֵל

יָד \ יָדַ֫יִם

וַיִּקַּח בְּיָדוֹ אֶת־הַמַּאֲכֶ֫לֶת

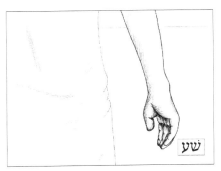

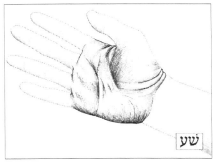

יָמִין

וַיִּשְׁלַח יִשְׂרָאֵל אֶת־יְמִינוֹ

כַּף \ כַּפּוֹת

וְיָצַק עַל־כַּף הַכֹּהֵן הַשְּׂמָאלִית

---

régel / ragláym
N: leg, foot (f)
And Sisera fled on his feet to the
tent of Jael. (Judg 4:17)

yamín
N: right hand, right (m)
And Israel reached out his right
hand. (Gen 48:14)

yád / yadáym
N: hand (f)
And he took in his hand the knife.
(Gen 22:6)

káf / kapót
N: palm (f)
And he shall pour (it) onto the palm
of the priest's left hand. (Lev 14:15)

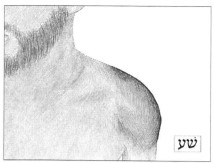

רֹאשׁ \ רָאשִׁים

וַהֲסִרֹתִי אֶת־רֹאשְׁךָ מֵעָלֶיךָ

כָּתֵף \ כְּתֵפַיִם

וַיָּשֶׂם אֹתָם עַל כִּתְפֹת הָאֵפֹד

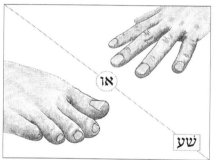

בֶּרֶךְ \ בִּרְכַּיִם

כָּרְעוּ עַל־בִּרְכֵיהֶם לִשְׁתּוֹת מַיִם

אֶצְבַּע \ אֶצְבָּעוֹת

וַיִּטְבֹּל אֶצְבָּעוֹ בַּדָּם

---

rósh / rashím
N: head (m)
"And I will remove your head from
upon you." (1 Sam 17:46)

katéf / kətafáym
N: shoulder (f)
And he placed them on the
shoulders of the ephod. (Exod 39:7)

bérex / birkáym
N: knee (f)
They bent down on their knees to
drink water. (Judg 7:6)

etsbá / etsba'ót
N: finger; toe (f)
And he dipped his finger in the
blood. (Lev 9:9)

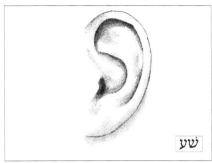

עַיִן \ עֵינַיִם

וְנֹחַ מָצָא חֵן בְּעֵינֵי יְהֹוָה

אֹזֶן \ אָזְנַיִם

וַיְדַבְּרוּ עַבְדֵי שָׁאוּל בְּאָזְנֵי דָוִד

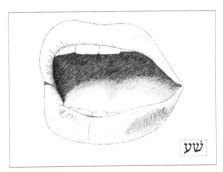

פֶּה

וְעַתָּה לֵךְ וְאָנֹכִי אֶהְיֶה עִם־פִּיךָ

אַף \ אַפַּיִם

וַיִּשְׁתַּחוּ אַפַּיִם אָרְצָה

áyn / enáym
N: eye (f)
But Noah found favor in the eyes of
YHWH. (Gen 6:8)

pé
N: mouth (m)
"And now, go, and I will be with
your mouth." (Exod 4:12)

ózen / oznáym
N: ear (f)
And the servants of Saul spoke in
the ears of David. (1 Sam 18:23)

áf / apáym
N: nose, nostrils; anger (m)
And he bowed down, nostrils to the
earth. (Gen 19:1)

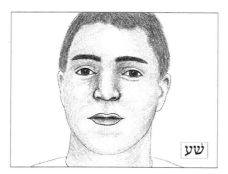

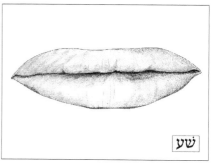

פָּנִים

וַיִּפֹּל אַבְרָם עַל־פָּנָיו

שָׂפָה \ שְׂפָתַיִם

מוֹצָא שְׂפָתֶיךָ תִּשְׁמֹר וְעָשִׂיתָ

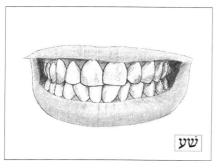

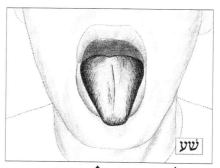

שֵׁן \ שִׁנַּיִם

עַיִן תַּחַת עַיִן שֵׁן תַּחַת שֵׁן

לָשׁוֹן \ לְשׁוֹנוֹת

כִּי כְבַד־פֶּה וּכְבַד לָשׁוֹן אָנֹכִי

---

paním
N: face (f)
And Abram fell on his face.
(Gen 17:3)

safá / sfatáym
N: lip (f)
"What has gone out of your lips you
shall keep and do." (Deut 23:24*)

shén / shináym
N: tooth (f)
"... an eye in place of an eye, a tooth
in place of a tooth." (Exod 21:24)

lashón / ləshonót
N: tongue (f)
"... because heavy of mouth and
heavy of tongue am I." (Exod 4:10)

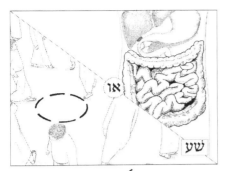

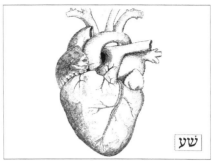

קֶ֫רֶב

לֵב · לֵבָב

הַחֵ֫לֶב הַמְכַסֶּה אֶת־הַקֶּ֫רֶב

כָּבֵד לֵב פַּרְעֹה מֵאֵן לְשַׁלַּח הָעָם

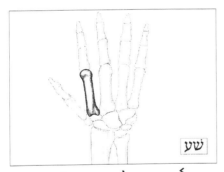

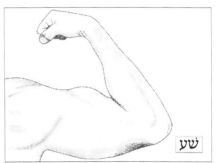

עֶ֫צֶם \ עֲצָמוֹת

כֹּחַ

זֹאת הַפַּ֫עַם עֶ֫צֶם מֵעֲצָמַי

הַגִּ֫ידָה־נָּא לִי בַּמֶּה כֹחֲךָ גָדוֹל

qérev
N: entrails; midst (m)
"... the fat that covers the entrails."
(Exod 29:22)

étsem / atsamót
N: bone (f)
"This one is this time bone of my
bones." (Gen 2:23)

lév / leváv
N: heart (m)
"Heavy is Pharaoh's heart. He refused
to send away the people." (Exod 7:14)

kóax
N: strength, power (m)
"Tell me, please. How is your
strength great?" (Judg 16:6)

2.2
Food

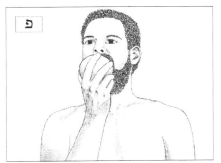

אָכַל \ יֹאכַל

אָדָם אֹכֵל אֶת־הַפְּרִי

אכל | וַיֹּאכַל | אֹכֵל | אָכַל

שָׁתָה \ יִשְׁתֶּה

הָעָם שָׁתָה מַיִם מִן־הַצּוּר

שתה | וַיֵּשְׁתְּ | שֹׁתֶה | שָׁתוֹת

טָעַם \ יִטְעַם

יוֹנָתָן טָעַם מְעַט דְּבַשׁ

טעם | וַיִּטְעַם | טֹעֵם | טָעַם

בָּלַע \ יִבְלַע

מַטֵּה־אַהֲרֹן בָּלַע אֶת־מַטֹּתָם

בלע | וַיִּבְלַע | בֹּלֵעַ | בָּלַע

---

axál / yoxál
Q: eat
Adam is eating the fruit.
(Gen 3:6)

ta'ám / yit'ám
Q: taste
Jonathan is tasting a little honey.
(1 Sam 14:43)

shatá / yishté
Q: drink
The people are drinking water from
the rock. (Exod 17:6)

balá / yivlá
Q: swallow
Aaron's staff is swallowing their
staffs. (Exod 7:12)

מִשְׁתֶּה

וַיַּעַשׂ לָהֶם מִשְׁתֶּה וַיֹּאכְלוּ וַיִּשְׁתּוּ

רָעָב

וַיְהִי רָעָב בָּאָרֶץ וַיֵּרֶד מִצְרַיְמָה

לֶחֶם

וּבְכָל־אֶרֶץ מִצְרַיִם הָיָה לֶחֶם

בָּשָׂר

כָּל־בָּשָׂר אֲשֶׁר־בּוֹ רוּחַ חַיִּים

---

mishté
N: feast, drinking (m)
He made them a feast, and they ate
and drank. (Gen 26:30)

ra'áv
N: famine, hunger (m)
There was a famine in the land, and
he went down to Egypt. (Gen 12:10)

léxem
N: bread (m)
But in all the land of Egypt there
was bread. (Gen 41:54)

basár
N: meat, flesh (m)
"... all flesh in which there is a spirit
of life." (Gen 6:17)

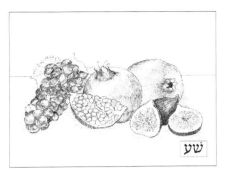

פְּרִי

וּבֵרַךְ פְּרִי־בִטְנְךָ וּפְרִי־אַדְמָתֶךָ

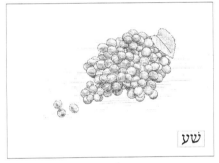

עֵנָב \ עֲנָבִים

וַיִּכְרְתוּ מִשָּׁם אֶשְׁכּוֹל עֲנָבִים

זֶרַע

תֶּן־זֶרַע וְנִחְיֶה וְלֹא נָמוּת

יַיִן

וּמַלְכִּי־צֶדֶק הוֹצִיא לֶחֶם וָיָיִן

---

prí
N: fruit; offspring (m)
"He will bless the fruit of your womb
and of your ground." (Deut 7:13)

zéra
N: seed; offspring (m)
"Give (us) seed, that we might live
and not die." (Gen 47:19)

enáv / anavím
N: grape (m)
From there they cut a cluster of
grapes. (Num 13:23)

yáyn
N: wine (m)
And Melchizedek brought out bread
and wine. (Gen 14:18)

2.3
Clothing

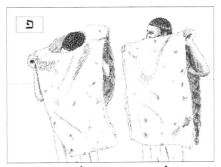

לָבַשׁ \ יִלְבַּשׁ

אַנְשֵׁי נִינְוֵה לֹבְשִׁים שַׂקִּים

לָבַשׁ | לָבֵשׁ | וַיִּלְבַּשׁ | לבש

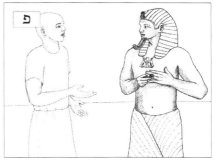

הֵסִיר \ יָסִיר

פַּרְעֹה מֵסִיר טַבַּעְתּוֹ מֵעַל יָדוֹ

הָסִיר | הָסֵר | וַיָּסַר | סור

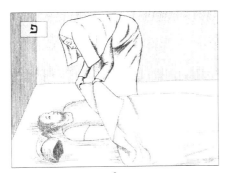

כִּסָּה \ יְכַסֶּה

יָעֵל מְכַסָּה אֶת־סִיסְרָא בַּשְּׂמִיכָה

כַּסּוּת | כַּסֶּה | וַיְכַס | כסה

גִּלָּה \ יְגַלֶּה

רוּת מְגַלָּה אֶת־מַרְגְּלֹת בֹּעַז

גַּלּוּת | גַּל | וַיְגַל | גלה

---

laváash / yilbáash
Q: put on, wear
The men of Nineveh are putting on
sackcloth. (Jon 3:5)

hesír / yasír
HI: remove
Pharaoh is removing his ring from
his hand. (Gen 41:42)

kisá / yəxasé
PI: cover
Jael is covering Sisera with the rug.
(Judg 4:18)

gilá / yəgalé
PI: uncover
Ruth is uncovering the place of
Boaz's feet. (Ruth 3:7)

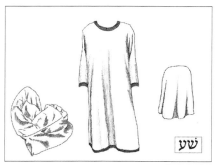

בֶּגֶד \ בְּגָדִים

וַתִּלְבַּשׁ בִּגְדֵי אַלְמְנוּתָהּ

אֵפוֹד

וַיַּעַשׂ אֶת־הָאֵפֹד זָהָב וְאַרְגָּמָן

שִׂמְלָה \ שְׂמָלוֹת

וַיִּקְרַע יַעֲקֹב שִׂמְלֹתָיו

מְעִיל \ מְעִילִים

וַיַּחֲזֵק שָׁאוּל בִּכְנַף־מְעִילוֹ וַיִּקְרַע

---

béged / bəgadím
N: clothes, cloth (m)
And she put on the clothes of her
widowhood. (Gen 38:19)

efód
N: ephod (m)
And he made the ephod out of gold
and of purple wool. (Exod 39:2)

simlá / smalót
N: outer garment (f)
And Jacob tore his garments.
(Gen 37:34)

məʾíl / məʾilím
N: robe, coat (m)
And Saul seized the edge of his
robe, and it tore. (1 Sam 15:27)

טַבַּעַת \ טַבָּעוֹת

וַיַּחְתֹּם בְּטַבַּעַת הַמֶּלֶךְ

עֲטָרָה \ עֲטָרוֹת

וַיִּקַּח אֶת־עֲטֶרֶת־מַלְכָּם

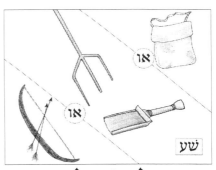

נַעַל \ נַעֲלַיִם

שַׁל־נְעָלֶיךָ מֵעַל רַגְלֶיךָ

כְּלִי \ כֵּלִים

וַיִּשְׁלַח דָּוִד אֶת־יָדוֹ אֶל־הַכְּלִי

---

tabá'at / taba'ót
N: ring, signet ring (f)
And he sealed (it) with the ring of
the king. (Esth 8:10)

atará / atarót
N: garland, crown (f)
And he took the crown of their king.
(2 Sam 12:30)

ná'al / na'aláym
N: sandal (f)
"Loosen your sandals from upon
your feet." (Exod 3:5)

klí / kelím
N: vessel; implement; weapon (m)
And David reached out his hand
into the bag. (1 Sam 17:49)

3
The Social Order

3.1
Family and Tribe

יָלַד \ יֵלֵד

שָׂרָה יָלְדָה לְאַבְרָהָם בֵּן

יָלַד | וַיֵּלֶד | — | לֶדֶת

הִרְבָּה \ יַרְבֶּה

יְהוָה מַרְבֶּה אֶת־זֶרַע אַבְרָהָם

רבה | וַיֶּרֶב | הֶרֶב/הִרְבָּה | הַרְבּוֹת

הוֹלִיד \ יוֹלִיד

אַבְרָהָם מוֹלִיד אֶת־יִצְחָק

יָלַד | וַיּוֹלֶד | הוֹלֵד | הוֹלִיד

גָּאַל \ יִגְאַל

בֹּעַז גָּאַל אֶת־הַשָּׂדֶה וְאֶת־רוּת

גאל | וַיִּגְאַל | גָּאַל | גְּאֹל

---

yalád / yeléd
Q: give birth
Sarah gives birth to a son for
Abraham. (Gen 21:2)

holíd / yolíd
HI: beget
Abraham begets Isaac.
(Gen 25:19)

hirbá / yarbé
HI: make many, multiply
YHWH multiplies the offspring of
Abraham. (Gen 26:4)

ga'ál / yig'ál
Q: redeem, buy back
Boaz is redeeming the field and
Ruth. (Ruth 4:6)

מִשְׁפָּחָה \ מִשְׁפָּחוֹת

וְנִבְרְכוּ בְךָ כֹּל מִשְׁפְּחֹת הָאֲדָמָה

דּוֹר \ דּוֹרוֹת

וַיָּמָת יוֹסֵף וְכֹל הַדּוֹר הַהוּא

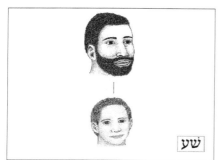

אָב \ אָבוֹת

וְחָם הוּא אֲבִי כְנָעַן

אֵם \ אִמּוֹת

יַעֲזָב־אִישׁ אֶת־אָבִיו וְאֶת־אִמּוֹ

---

mishpaxá / mishpaxót
N: family, clan (f)
"And in you will be blessed all the
families of the ground." (Gen 12:3)

dór / dorót
N: generation (m)
Joseph died, and all of that
generation. (Exod 1:6)

áv / avót
N: father (m)
And Ham was the father of Canaan.
(Gen 9:18)

ém / imót
N: mother (f)
A man shall leave his father and his
mother. (Gen 2:24)

בֵּן \ בָּנִים

וַיֵּדַע אָדָם אֶת־אִשְׁתּוֹ וַתֵּלֶד בֵּן

בַּת \ בָּנוֹת

קַח אֶת־אִשְׁתְּךָ וְאֶת־שְׁתֵּי בְנֹתֶיךָ

אָח \ אָחִים

וַיֹּאמֶר קַיִן אֶל־הֶבֶל אָחִיו

אָחוֹת \ אֲחָיוֹת

לָמָה אָמַרְתָּ אֲחֹתִי הִיא

---

bén / baním
N: son (m)
Adam knew his wife, and she bore a
son. (Gen 4:25)

áx / axím
N: brother (m)
And Cain said to Abel his brother ...
(Gen 4:8)

bát / banót
N: daughter (f)
"Take your wife and your two
daughters." (Gen 19:15)

axót / axayót
N: sister (f)
"Why did you say, 'She is my
sister'?" (Gen 12:19)

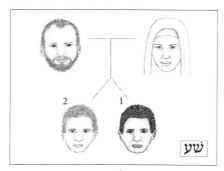

בְּכוֹר \ בְּכוֹרִים

וַיֹּאמֶר אֲנִי בִּנְךָ בְכֹרְךָ עֵשָׂו

נַחֲלָה \ נְחָלוֹת

נַחֲלָתוֹ הִיא לְבָנָיו תִּהְיֶה

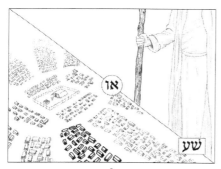

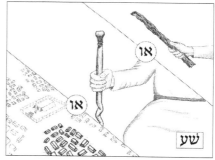

מַטֶּה \ מַטּוֹת

וְאֶת־הַמַּטֶּה הַזֶּה תִּקַּח בְּיָדֶךָ

שֵׁבֶט \ שְׁבָטִים

וְשֵׁבֶט לְגֵו כְּסִילִים

---

bəxór / bəxorím
N: firstborn (m)
And he said, "I am your son, your
firstborn, Esau." (Gen 27:32)

naxalá / nəxalót
N: inheritance (f)
"It is his inheritance. It shall belong
to his sons." (Ezek 46:16)

maté / matót
N: staff; tribe (m)
"And this staff you shall take in your
hand." (Exod 4:17)

shévet / shvatím
N: rod, scepter; tribe (m)
And a rod is for the back of fools.
(Prov 26:3)

אָדוֹן \ אֲדֹנִים

וַיִּקַּח הָעֶבֶד עֲשָׂרָה גְמַלֵּי אֲדֹנָיו

עֶבֶד \ עֲבָדִים

עֲבָדִים הָיִינוּ לְפַרְעֹה בְּמִצְרָיִם

נָשִׂיא \ נְשִׂיאִים

וְנָשִׂיא לִבְנֵי יְהוּדָה נַחְשׁוֹן

רֵעַ \ רֵעִים

לֹא תַחְמֹד בֵּית רֵעֶךָ

---

adón / adoním
N: lord, master (m)
And the servant took ten of his
master's camels. (Gen 24:10)

éved / avadím
N: slave, servant (m)
"Slaves we were to Pharaoh in
Egypt." (Deut 6:21)

nasí / nəsi'ím
N: leader, prince (m)
And the leader for the children of
Judah was Nahshon. (Num 2:3)

réa / re'ím
N: neighbor, friend (m)
"You shall not desire the house of
your neighbor." (Exod 20:17)

3.2
Personal Interactions

שָׁאַל \ יִשְׁאַל

הָעָם שֹׁאֲלִים מִשְׁמוּאֵל מֶלֶךְ

שאל | וַיִּשְׁאַל | שָׁאַל | שָׁאַל

עָנָה \ יַעֲנֶה

אֶסְתֵּר עָנָה אֶת־הַמֶּלֶךְ

ענה | וַיַּעַן | עָנֶה | עָנוֹת

בָּקֵשׁ \ יְבַקֵּשׁ

שָׁאוּל מְבַקֵּשׁ אֶת־דָּוִד

בקש | וַיְבַקֵּשׁ | בָּקֵשׁ | בַּקֵּשׁ

מָצָא \ יִמְצָא

הַכֹּהֵן מָצָא אֶת־סֵפֶר הַתּוֹרָה

מצא | וַיִּמְצָא | מָצָא | מְצֹא

---

sha'ál / yish'ál
Q: ask
The people are asking for a king
from Samuel. (1 Sam 8:10)

biqésh / yəvaqésh
PI: seek, look for
Saul is looking for David.
(1 Sam 23:14)

aná / ya'ané
Q: answer
Esther is answering the king.
(Esth 5:7)

matsá / yimtsá
Q: find
The priest finds the Book of the
Law. (2 Kgs 22:8)

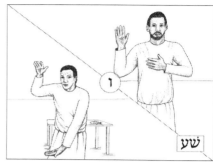

קוֹל \ קוֹלוֹת

וַיְמֻשֵּׁהוּ וַיֹּאמֶר הַקֹּל קוֹל יַעֲקֹב

אֱמֶת · שֶׁקֶר

אֱמֶת לֹא יְדַבֵּרוּ לִמְּדוּ לְשׁוֹנָם שֶׁקֶר

שָׁלוֹם \ שְׁלוֹמִים

שָׁלוֹם לְךָ אַל־תִּירָא לֹא תָּמוּת

חֵמָה

עַד אֲשֶׁר־תָּשׁוּב חֲמַת אָחִיךָ

---

qól / qolót
N: voice, noise (m)
He felt him and said, "The voice is
the voice of Jacob." (Gen 27:22)

emét / shéqer
N: truth, faithfulness; lie
"Truth they do not speak; they have
taught their tongue a lie." (Jer 9:4*)

shalóm / shlomím
N: peace (m)
"Peace to you. Do not fear—you will
not die." (Judg 6:23)

xemá
N: wrath (f)
"... until the wrath of your brother
returns." (Gen 27:44)

הִגִּיד \ יַגִּיד

שִׁמְשׁוֹן מַגִּיד לִדְלִילָה עַל־שְׂעָרוֹ

נגד | וַיַּגֵּד | הַגֵּד | הַגִּיד

סִפֵּר \ יְסַפֵּר

יוֹסֵף מְסַפֵּר חֲלוֹם לְאֶחָיו

ספר | וַיְסַפֵּר | סַפֵּר | סִפֵּר

נִבָּא \ יִנָּבֵא

יִרְמְיָהוּ נִבָּא בַּחֲצַר בֵּית־יְהוָה

נבא | וַיִּנָּבֵא | הִנָּבֵא | הִנָּבֵא

נִשְׁבַּע \ יִשָּׁבַע

עֵשָׂו נִשְׁבַּע לִמְכֹּר בְּכֹרָתוֹ לְיַעֲקֹב

שבע | וַיִּשָּׁבַע | הִשָּׁבַע | הִשָּׁבַע

higíd / yagíd
HI: tell, inform
Samson is telling Delilah about his hair. (Judg 16:17)

nibá / yinavé
NI: prophesy
Jeremiah is prophesying in the court of YHWH's house. (Jer 19:14)

sipér / yəsapér
PI: recount, give the details
Joseph is recounting a dream for his brothers. (Gen 37:9)

nishbá / yishavá
NI: swear
Esau is swearing to sell his birthright to Jacob. (Gen 25:33)

קָהָל

וַיַּקְהִֽלוּ מֹשֶׁה וְאַהֲרֹן אֶת־הַקָּהָל

עֵדָה

וְלֹא־הָיָה מַיִם לָעֵדָה

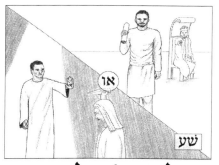

מַלְאָךְ \ מַלְאָכִים

וַיִּשְׁלַח שָׁאוּל מַלְאָכִים אֶל־יִשַׁי

נְאֻם

וְקַמְתִּי עֲלֵיהֶם נְאֻם יְהוָה

---

qahál
N: assembly (m)
Moses and Aaron assembled the
assembly. (Num 20:10)

edáh
N: congregation (f)
But there was no water for the
congregation. (Num 20:2)

mal'áx / mal'axím
N: messenger; angel (m)
And Saul sent messengers to Jesse.
(1 Sam 16:19)

nə'úm
N: declaration
"And I will rise up against them," the
declaration of YHWH. (Isa 14:22)

פָּקַד \ יִפְקֹד

דָּוִד פָּקֵד אֶת־אֶחָיו לְשָׁלוֹם

פקד | וַיִּפְקֹד | פָּקַד | פְּקֹד

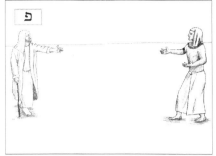

לִקְרַאת

*יוֹסֵף עָלָה לִקְרַאת יִשְׂרָאֵל אָבִיו

קרא | 95% of this root's instances are in the above infintive form

שָׁלַח \ יִשְׁלַח

בַּת־פַּרְעֹה שֹׁלַחַת אֶת־אֲמָתָהּ

שלח | וַיִּשְׁלַח | שָׁלַח | שְׁלַח

נָטָה \ יִטֶּה

מֹשֶׁה נֹטֶה אֶת־יָדוֹ עַל־הַיָּם

נטה | וַיֵּט | נָטָה | נְטוֹת

---

paqád / yifqód
Q: visit; list, look after; appoint
David is visiting his brothers to see
if they are well. (1 Sam 17:18)

liqrát
Q: meet, encounter
Joseph is going up to meet Israel his
father. (Gen 46:29)

shaláx / yíshlax
Q: send
The daughter of Pharaoh is sending
her servant girl. (Exod 2:5)

natá / yité
Q: stretch out; turn
Moses is stretching out his hand
upon the sea. (Exod 14:21)

3.3
Worship/Cultic

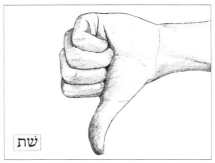

טוֹב \ טוֹבָה

וַיַּרְא אֱלֹהִים וְהִנֵּה־טוֹב מְאֹד

רַע \ רָעָה

הָיָה כְּאַחַד מִמֶּנּוּ לָדַעַת טוֹב וָרַע

צַדִּיק \ צַדִּיקָה

נֹחַ אִישׁ צַדִּיק

רָשָׁע \ רִשְׁעָה

הַאַף תִּסְפֶּה צַדִּיק עִם־רָשָׁע

tóv / tová
ADJ: good (m/f)
God saw and, behold, it was very
good. (Gen 1:31)

tsadíq / tsadiqá
ADJ: righteous, just (m/f)
Noah was a righteous man.
(Gen 6:9)

rá / ra'á
ADJ: bad, evil (m/f)
"He has become like one of us,
knowing good and evil." (Gen 3:22)

rashá / rəsha'á
ADJ: guilty, wicked (m/f)
"Will you indeed sweep away
righteous with wicked?" (Gen 18:23)

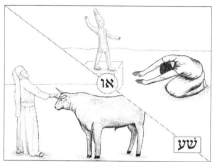

תּוֹעֵבָה \ תּוֹעֵבוֹת

יַעֲשֶׂה פֶּסֶל תּוֹעֲבַת יְהוָה

חַטָּאת \ חַטֹּאת

אֲכַפְּרָה בְּעַד חַטַּאתְכֶם

עָוֹן \ עֲוֹנוֹת

שָׁבוּ עַל־עֲוֹנֹת אֲבוֹתָם הָרִאשֹׁנִים

בַּעַל \ בְּעָלִים

וּבַעַל הַשּׁוֹר נָקִי

---

to'evá / to'evót
N: abomination (f)
"He makes an idol, an abomination
to Yahweh." (Deut 27:15)

avón / avonót
N: transgression, iniquity (m)
"They have returned to the iniquities
of their first fathers." (Jer 11:10)

xatát / xatót
N: sin; sin offering (f)
"I shall atone for your sin."
(Exod 32:30)

bá'al / bə'alím
N: owner, husband; Baal (m)
"But the owner of the ox is
innocent." (Exod 21:28)

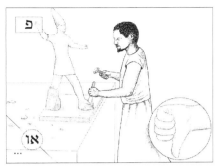

הֵרֵע \ יָרַע

הָעֹשֶׂה פֶּסֶל מֵרַע

הָרַע | וַיָּרַע | — | רעע

חָטָא \ יֶחֱטָא

עָכָן חֹטֵא לַיהוָה

חָטָא | — | וַיֶּחֱטָא | חטא

חִלֵּל \ יְחַלֵּל

הַנֹּתֵן לַמֹּלֶךְ מְחַלֵּל אֶת־שֵׁם יְהוָה

חִלֵּל | — | וַיְחַלֵּל | חלל

טָמֵא \ יִטְמָא

הַחֲזִיר טָמֵא לַבָּנִים אֲשֶׁר לַיהוָה

טָמְאָה | — | וַיִּטְמָא | טמא

---

herá / yará
HI: do evil
The one who makes an idol does an evil thing. (1 Kgs 14:9)

xilél / yəxalél
PI: profane
The one who gives to Molech profanes YHWH's name. (Lev 20:3)

xatá / yexetá
Q: sin
Achan is sinning against YHWH. (Josh 7:20)

tamé / yitmá
Q: be unclean
The pig is unclean for the children that belong to YHWH. (Deut 14:8)

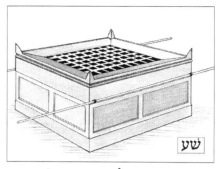

זֶבַח \ זְבָחִים

וְאֶת־הָאַיִל יַעֲשֶׂה זֶבַח שְׁלָמִים

מִזְבֵּחַ \ מִזְבְּחוֹת

וַיִּבֶן שָׁם אַבְרָהָם אֶת־הַמִּזְבֵּחַ

עֹלָה \ עֹלוֹת

וְכֶבֶשׂ בֶּן־שְׁנָתוֹ תַּעֲשֶׂה עוֹלָה

מִנְחָה \ מְנָחוֹת

מִנְחָה הִיא שְׁלוּחָה לַאדֹנִי לְעֵשָׂו

---

zévax / zvaxím
N: sacrifice (m)
"And the ram he shall make as a
sacrifice of peace." (Num 6:17)

mizbéax / mizbəxót
N: altar (m)
And Abraham built the altar there.
(Gen 22:9)

olá / olót
N: whole burnt offering (f)
"A year old sheep you shall make as a
whole burnt offering." (Ezek 46:13)

minxá / minxót
N: gift, offering (f)
"It is a gift sent to my lord, to Esau."
(Gen 32:19*)

זֶבַח \ יִזְבַּח

הַמַּלָּחִים זֹבְחִים זֶבַח לַיהוָה

זֶבַח | וַיִּזְבַּח | זֶבַח | זבח

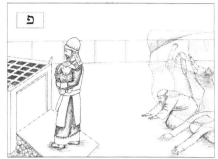

כִּפֶּר \ יְכַפֵּר

אַהֲרֹן מְכַפֵּר בַּעֲדוֹ וּבְעַד הָעָם

כַּפֵּר | כִּפֶּר | וַיְכַפֵּר | כפר

שָׂרַף \ יִשְׂרֹף

מֹשֶׁה שָׂרַף אֶת־הָעֵגֶל בָּאֵשׁ

שָׂרַף | שָׂרֹף | וַיִּשְׂרֹף | שרף

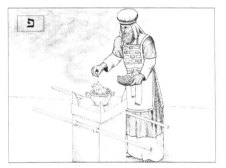

הִקְטִיר \ יַקְטִיר

אַהֲרֹן מַקְטִיר קְטֹרֶת סַמִּים

הַקְטִיר | הַקְטֵר | וַיַּקְטֵר | קטר

---

zaváx / yizbáx
Q: slaughter, sacrifice
The sailors are sacrificing a sacrifice
to YHWH. (Jon 1:16)

kipér / yəxapér
PI: atone, cover
Aaron is atoning for himself and for
the people. (Lev 16:24)

saráf / yisróf
Q: burn
Moses is burning the calf with fire.
(Exod 32:20)

hiqtír / yaqtír
HI: make smoke (incense/sacrifice)
Aaron is burning an incense of
spices. (Exod 30:7)

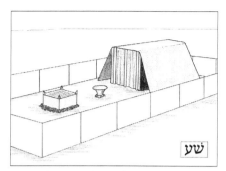

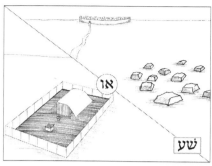

מִשְׁכָּן \ מִשְׁכָּנוֹת

וַיָּבֵא אֶת־הָאָרֹן אֶל־הַמִּשְׁכָּן

חָצֵר \ חֲצֵרוֹת

עָרִים שְׁתַּיִם וְחַצְרֵיהֶן

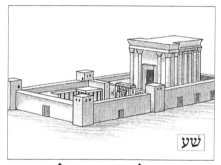

הֵיכָל \ הֵיכָלוֹת

וְהוּא יִבְנֶה אֶת־הֵיכַל יְהוָה

עַמּוּד \ עַמּוּדִים

וַיָּקֶם אֶת־הָעַמֻּדִים לְאֻלָם הַהֵיכָל

---

mishkán / mishkanót
N: tabernacle (f)
And he brought the ark into the
tabernacle. (Exod 40:21)

hexál / hexalót
N: temple; palace (m)
"And he will build the temple of
YHWH." (Zech 6:13)

xatsér / xatserót
N: village; courtyard (f)
... two cities and their villages.
(Josh 15:60)

amúd / amudím
N: pillar (m)
And he raised the pillars for the
porch of the temple. (1 Kgs 7:21)

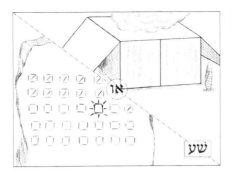

מוֹעֵד \ מוֹעֲדִים
וַיָּשֶׂם אֶת־הַמְּנֹרָה בְּאֹהֶל מוֹעֵד

אָרוֹן
וְעָשׂוּ אֲרוֹן עֲצֵי שִׁטִּים

בָּמָה \ בָּמוֹת
וַיִּבְנוּ גַם־הֵמָּה לָהֶם בָּמוֹת

חוּץ \ חוּצוֹת
וַיִּשְׂרְפֵם מִחוּץ לִירוּשָׁלַם

---

mo'éd / mo'adím
N: appointed place/time (m)
He placed the lampstand in the tent
of meeting. (Exod 40:24)

bamá / bamót
N: (cultic) high place (f)
And they also built for themselves
high places. (1 Kgs 14:23)

arón
N: chest, ark (m)
"And they shall make an ark of wood
from acacia trees." (Exod 25:10)

xúts / xutsót
N: outside (sg); streets (pl)
And they burned them outside of
Jerusalem. (2 Kgs 23:4)

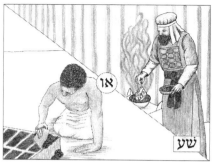

כֹּהֵן \ כֹּהֲנִים

וְלָקַח הַכֹּהֵן הַמָּשִׁיחַ מִדַּם הַפָּר

עֲבֹדָה

לַעֲבֹד אֶת־עֲבֹדָתָם בְּאֹהֶל מוֹעֵד

דָּם \ דָּמִים

וַיִּטְבְּלוּ אֶת־הַכֻּתֹּנֶת בַּדָּם

שֶׁמֶן \ שְׁמָנִים

וְלָקַחְתָּ אֶת־שֶׁמֶן הַמִּשְׁחָה

---

kohén / kohaním
N: priest (m)
"The anointed priest shall take from
the blood of the bull." (Lev 4:5)

dám / damím
N: blood (m)
And they dipped the tunic in the
blood. (Gen 37:31)

avodá
N: service; work, slavery (f)
... to perform their service in the
tent of meeting. (Num 8:22)

shémen / shmaním
N: oil (m)
"And you shall take the oil of the
annointing." (Exod 29:7)

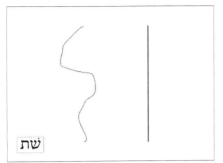

יָשָׁר \ יְשָׁרָה

וַיַּדְרִיכֵם בְּדֶרֶךְ יְשָׁרָה

קָדוֹשׁ \ קְדֹשָׁה

וִהְיִיתֶם לִי קְדֹשִׁים כִּי קָדוֹשׁ אֲנִי

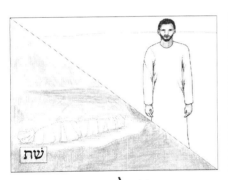

חַי \ חַיָּה

וַיַּגִּדוּ לוֹ לֵאמֹר עוֹד יוֹסֵף חַי

חָכָם \ חֲכָמָה

הִנֵּה נָתַתִּי לְךָ לֵב חָכָם וְנָבוֹן

---

yashár / yǝshará
ADJ: straight, (up)right (m/f)
"And he made them tread in a
straight path." (Ps 107:7)

qadósh / qǝdoshá
ADJ: holy (m/f)
"You shall be holy to me, because I
am holy." (Lev 20:26)

xáy / xayá
ADJ: alive, living (m/f)
And they told him, saying, "Joseph
is still alive." (Gen 45:26)

xaxám / xaxamá
ADJ: wise (m/f)
"Behold, I give to you a wise and
discerning heart." (1 Kgs 3:12)

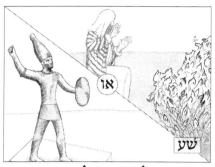

אֵל \ אֱלֹהִים   יְהוָה

YHWH

וַיְדַבֵּר אֱלֹהִים אֶל־מֹשֶׁה אֲנִי יְהוָה   אָנֹכִי אֱלֹהֵי אָבִיךָ אֱלֹהֵי אַבְרָהָם

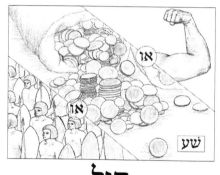

כָּבוֹד   חַיִל

כִּי־מָלֵא הַכָּבוֹד אֶת־בֵּית יְהוָה   וַתָּבֹא יְרוּשָׁלַמָה בְּחַיִל כָּבֵד מְאֹד

él / elohím
N: God; god (m)
"I am the God of your father, the
God of Abraham." (Exod 3:6)

adonáy
N: (God's covenant name) (m)
And God said to Moses, "I am
YHWH." (Exod 6:2)

kavód
N: glory (m)
... because the glory filled the house
of YHWH. (1 Kgs 8:11)

xáyl
N: strength; wealth; army (m)
And she came to Jerusalem with very
much wealth. (1 Kgs 10:2)

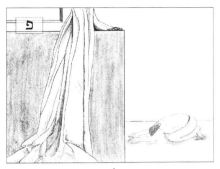

רָם \ יָרוּם

רָם אֲדֹנָי אֲשֶׁר עַל־כִּסֵּא

רום | וַיָּרָם | רום | רום

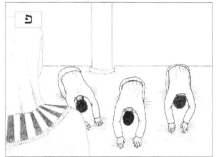

הִשְׁתַּחֲוָה \ יִשְׁתַּחֲוֶה

אֲחֵי יוֹסֵף מִשְׁתַּחֲוִים לוֹ

חוה | וַיִּשְׁתַּחוּ | הִשְׁתַּחֲוֶה | הִשְׁתַּחֲוֺת

הוֹדָה \ יוֹדֶה

לֵאָה מוֹדָה אֶת־יְהוָה עַל־יְהוּדָה

ידה | — | הוֹדָה | הוֹדוֹת

הִלֵּל \ יְהַלֵּל

דָּוִד מְהַלֵּל אֶת־יְהוָה בְּתוֹךְ קָהָל

הלל | וַיְהַלֵּל | הַלֵּל | הַלֵּל

---

rám / yarúm
Q: be high, be exalted
The Lord is high who is on a throne.
(Isa 6:1)

hishtaxavá / yishtaxavé
HSTFL: bow down
Joseph's brothers are bowing down
to him. (Gen 42:6)

hodá / yodé
HI: thank, praise
Leah is thanking YHWH for Judah.
(Gen 29:35)

hilél / yəhalél
PI: praise
David is praising YHWH in the
midst of an assembly. (Ps 22:23*)

3.4
People, Law, and Covenant

מֶֽלֶךְ \ מְלָכִים

בֹּא דַבֵּר אֶל־פַּרְעֹה מֶֽלֶךְ מִצְרָֽיִם

מַמְלָכָה \ מַמְלָכוֹת

לֹא־אֶקַּח אֶת־כָּל־הַמַּמְלָכָה מִיָּדוֹ

גּוֹי \ גּוֹיִם

תִּהְיוּ מַמְלֶֽכֶת כֹּהֲנִים וְגוֹי קָדוֹשׁ

עַם \ עַמִּים

עַם בְּנֵי יִשְׂרָאֵל רַב וְעָצוּם מִמֶּֽנּוּ

---

mélex / mlaxím
N: king (m)
"Enter, speak to Phraoh, the king of
Egypt." (Exod 6:11)

góy / goyím
N: nation (m)
"You shall be a kingdom of priests
and a holy nation." (Exod 19:6)

mamlaxá / mamlaxót
N: kingdom (f)
"I will not take all of the kingdom
from his hand." (1 Kgs 11:34)

ám / amím
N: people (m)
"The people of the Israelites are too
many and strong for us." (Exod 1:9)

חֹק · חֻקָּה

וּשְׁמַרְתֶּם אֶת־הַמִּצְוֹת חֻקַּת עוֹלָם

מִצְוָה \ מִצְוֹת

מִצְוֹתָיו אֲשֶׁר־צִוָּה אֶת־מֹשֶׁה

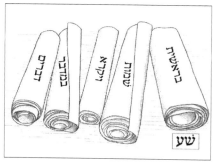

מִשְׁפָּט \ מִשְׁפָּטִים

וְשָׁאַל לוֹ בְּמִשְׁפַּט הָאוּרִים

תּוֹרָה \ תּוֹרוֹת

כַּכָּתוּב בְּתוֹרַת מֹשֶׁה

---

xóq / xuqá
N: statute, prescription (m/f)
"You shall keep the Unleavened Bread
as a statute forever." (Exod 12:17)

mitsvá / mitsvót
N: commandment (f)
"... his commandments that he
commanded Moses." (2 Kgs 18:6)

mishpát / mishpatím
N: judgment, decision (m)
"And he shall ask for him by the
judgment of the Urim." (Num 27:21)

torá / torót
N: law, instruction (f)
"... as it is written in the Law of
Moses." (1 Kgs 2:3)

שָׁמַר \ יִשְׁמֹר

כְּרֻבִים שֹׁמְרִים דֶּרֶךְ עֵץ הַחַיִּים

שָׁמַר | שָׁמֹר | וַיִּשְׁמֹר | שׁמר

צִוָּה \ יְצַוֶּה

מֹשֶׁה מְצַוֶּה אֶת־הָעָם יִשְׂרָאֵל

צַוֹּת | צַו\צַוֶּה | וַיְצַו | צוה

שָׁפַט \ יִשְׁפֹּט

שְׁלֹמֹה שֹׁפֵט בֵּין שְׁתַּיִם נָשִׁים

שָׁפַט | שָׁפֹט | וַיִּשְׁפֹּט | שׁפט

דָּרַשׁ \ יִדְרֹשׁ

שָׁאוּל דֹּרֵשׁ בְּאֵשֶׁת בַּעֲלַת־אוֹב

דָּרֹשׁ | דָּרֹשׁ | וַיִּדְרֹשׁ | דרשׁ

---

shamár / yishmór
Q: guard, keep
Cherubim are guarding the way to the tree of life. (Gen 3:24)

shafát / yishpót
Q: judge
Solomon is judging between two women. (1 Kgs 3:28)

tsivá / yətsavé
PI: command
Moses is commanding the people, Israel. (Deut 4:13)

darásh / yidrósh
Q: inquire, seek
Saul is inquiring of a female necromancer. (1 Sam 28:7)

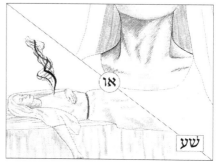

נֶֽפֶשׁ \ נְפָשׁוֹת

עֻנּוּ בַכֶּֽבֶל רַגְלָיו בַּרְזֶל בָּֽאָה נַפְשׁוֹ

חֶֽסֶד \ חֲסָדִים

הַנֶּאֱמָן שֹׁמֵר הַבְּרִית וְהַחֶֽסֶד

מְלָאכָה \ מְלָאכוֹת

שֵׁשֶׁת יָמִים תֵּעָשֶׂה מְלָאכָה

בְּרִית

וַיִּכְרְתוּ שְׁנֵיהֶם בְּרִית לִפְנֵי יְהוָה

---

xésed / xasadím
N: steadfast love (m)
"... the one who keeps the covenant
and the steadfast love." (Deut 7:9)

brít
N: covenant (f)
And the two of them cut a covenant
before YHWH. (1 Sam 23:18)

néfesh / nəfashót
N: throat; soul, living being (f)
"They oppressed his feet in a fetter;
his neck entered iron." (Ps 105:18)

mlaxá / mal'axót
N: work, occupation (f)
"Six days work shall be done."
(Exod 35:2)

זָכַר \ יִזְכֹּר

יוֹסֵף זָכַר אֶת הַחֲלוֹם

זכר | וַיִּזְכֹּר | זָכֹר | זָכַר

שָׁכַח \ יִשְׁכַּח

עֵשָׂו שָׁכַח אֶת אֲשֶׁר־עָשָׂה יַעֲקֹב

שכח | וַיִּשְׁכַּח | שָׁכַח | שָׁכַח

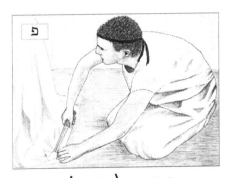

כָּרַת \ יִכְרֹת

דָּוִד כָּרַת אֶת־כְּנַף־מְעִיל שָׁאוּל

כרת | וַיִּכְרֹת | כָּרֹת | כָּרַת

שָׁבַר \ יִשְׁבֹּר

אַנְשֵׁי גִדְעוֹן שֹׁבְרִים כַּדִּים

שבר | וַיִּשְׁבֹּר | שָׁבֹר | שָׁבַר

---

zaxár / yizkór
Q: remember
Joseph remembers the dream.
(Gen 42:9)

shaxáx / yishkáx
Q: forget
Esau forgets what Jacob did.
(Gen 27:45)

karát / yixrót
Q: cut
David is cutting the corner of Saul's
robe. (1 Sam 24:5*)

shavár / yishbór
Q: break
The men of Gideon are breaking
pitchers. (Judg 7:20)

קַלֵּל \ יְקַלֵּל

שִׁמְעִי מְקַלֵּל אֶת־דָּוִד

קַלֵּל | קַלֵּל | וַיְקַלֵּל | קלל

בֵּרַךְ \ יְבָרֵךְ

יִצְחָק מְבָרֵךְ אֶת־יַעֲקֹב

בֵּרַךְ | בָּרֵךְ | וַיְבָרֶךְ | ברך

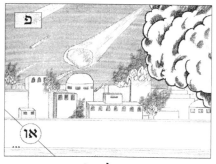

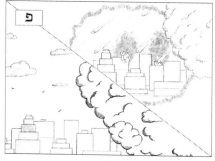

שִׁחֵת \ יְשַׁחֵת

אֱלֹהִים מְשַׁחֵת אֶת־סְדֹם

שַׁחֵת | שַׁחֵת | — | שחת

נִחַם \ יְנַחֵם

הָאֱלֹהִים נִחַם עַל־הָרָעָה לְנִינְוֵה

הַנַּחֵם | הַנַּחֵם | וַיִּנַּחֵם | נחם

---

qilél / yəqalél
PI: curse
Shimei is cursing David.
(2 Sam 19:22)

beráx / yəvaréx
PI: bless
Isaac is blessing Jacob.
(Gen 27:27)

shixét / yəshaxét
PI: ruin, destroy
God is destroying Sodom.
(Gen 19:29)

nixám / yinaxém
NI: regret, relent; be comforted
God relents concerning the disaster
against Nineveh. (Jon 3:10)

רָעָה \ יִרְעֶה

דָּוִד רֹעֶה אֶת־צֹאן אָבִיו

רעה | וַיִּרְעֶה | רֹעֶה | רְעוֹת

הוֹלִיךְ \ יוֹלִיךְ

מֹשֶׁה מוֹלִיךְ אֶת־הָעָם בְּתוֹךְ הַיָּם

הלך | וַיּוֹלֶךְ | הוֹלֵךְ | הוֹלִיךְ

הוֹשִׁיעַ \ יוֹשִׁיעַ

יְהוָה מוֹשִׁיעַ אֶת־יִשְׂרָאֵל

ישע | וַיּוֹשַׁע | הוֹשַׁע | הוֹשִׁיעַ

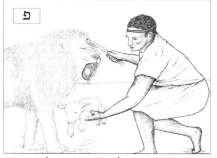

הִצִּיל \ יַצִּיל

דָּוִד מַצִּיל שֶׂה מִפִּי הָאֲרִי

נצל | וַיַּצֵּל | הַצֵּל | הַצִּיל

---

ra'á / yir'é
Q: tend; graze
David is shepherding the flock of his
father. (1 Sam 17:34)

hoshía / yoshía
HI: help, save
YHWH is saving Israel.
(Exod 14:30)

holíx / yolíx
HI: lead
Moses is leading the people in the
midst of the sea. (Ps 106:9)

hitsíl / yatsíl
HI: rescue
David is rescuing a lamb from the
mouth of the lion. (1 Sam 17:35)

3.5
Lands and Warfare

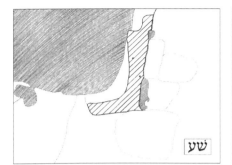

יִשְׂרָאֵל

וַיִּתֵּן לְיִשְׂרָאֵל אֶת־כָּל־הָאָרֶץ

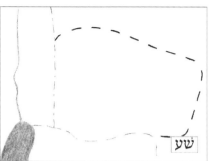

גְּבוּל \ גְּבוּלוֹת

וְזֶה־יִהְיֶה לָכֶם גְּבוּל צָפוֹן

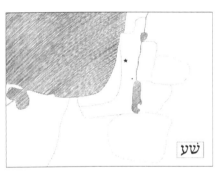

שֹׁמְרוֹן

מָלַךְ עַל־יִשְׂרָאֵל בְּשֹׁמְרוֹן

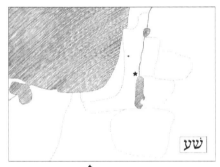

יְרוּשָׁלַם

שָׁלֹשׁ שָׁנִים מָלַךְ בִּירוּשָׁלַם

---

yisra'él
N: Israel (m)
And he gave to Israel all the land.
(Josh 21:43)

gvúl / gvulót
N: border (m)
"And this shall be for you a northern
border." (Num 34:7)

shomrón
N: Samaria (f)
He reigned over Israel in Samaria.
(1 Kgs 22:52*)

yərushaláym
N: Jerusalem (f)
Three years he reigned in Jerusalem.
(1 Kgs 15:2)

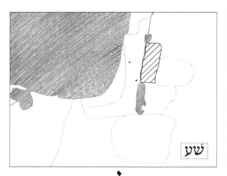

גִּלְעָד

וְאֶרֶץ הַגִּלְעָד הָיְתָה לִבְנֵי־מְנַשֶּׁה

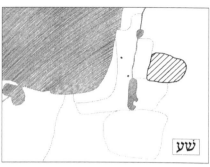

עַמּוֹן

וַיַּעַבְרוּ בְנֵי־עַמּוֹן אֶת־הַיַּרְדֵּן

אֱדוֹם

וַיְמָאֵן אֱדוֹם נְתֹן אֶת־יִשְׂרָאֵל עֲבֹר

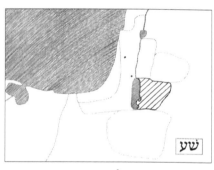

מוֹאָב

וַיֵּלֶךְ אִישׁ לָגוּר בִּשְׂדֵי מוֹאָב

---

gil'ád
N: Gilead
And the land of Gilead belonged to the children of Manasseh. (Josh 17:6)

edóm
N: Edom
And Edom refused to allow Israel to pass by. (Num 20:21)

amón
N: Ammon
And the children of Ammon crossed over the Jordan. (Judg 10:9)

mo'áv
N: Moab
A man went to dwell in the fields of Moab. (Ruth 1:1)

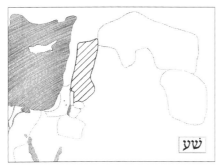

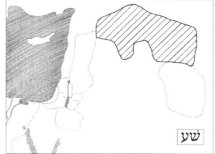

אֲרָם

וַיַּהֲרֹג מֵאֲרָם שְׁבַע מֵאוֹת רֶכֶב

אַשּׁוּר

וַיִּשְׁלַח חִזְקִיָּה אֶל־מֶֽלֶךְ־אַשּׁוּר

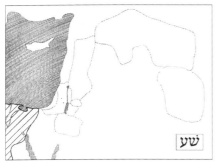

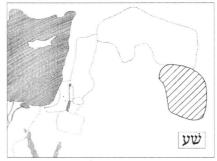

מִצְרַיִם

וַיֵּרֶד אַבְרָם מִצְרַיְמָה לָגוּר שָׁם

בָּבֶל

וַיָּבֹא מֶֽלֶךְ־בָּבֶל עַל־הָעִיר

---

arám
N: Aram
And he slayed from Aram 700
chariots. (2 Sam 10:18)

ashúr
N: Assyria
And Hezekiah sent to the king of
Assyria. (2 Kgs 18:14)

mitsráym
N: Egypt
And Abram went down to Egypt to
dwell there. (Gen 12:10)

bavél
N: Babylon (Babel)
And the king of Babylon came
against the city. (2 Kgs 24:11)

מִלְחָמָה \ מִלְחָמוֹת

וַיֵּצֵא לִקְרַאת פְּלִשְׁתִּים לַמִּלְחָמָה

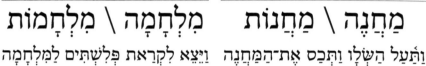

מַחֲנֶה \ מַחֲנוֹת

וַתַּעַל הַשְּׂלָו וַתְּכַס אֶת־הַמַּחֲנֶה

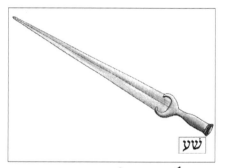

חֶרֶב \ חֲרָבוֹת

וַיַּעַשׂ לוֹ אֵהוּד חֶרֶב

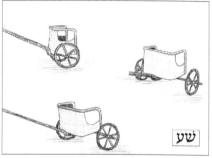

רֶכֶב

וַיָּשֻׁבוּ הַמַּיִם וַיְכַסּוּ אֶת־הָרֶכֶב

---

milxamá / milxamót
N: battle, war (f)
He went out to meet the
Philistines for battle. (1 Sam 4:1)

maxané / maxanót
N: camp (m)
The quail came up and covered the
camp. (Exod 16:13)

xérev / xaravót
N: sword (f)
And Ehud made for himself a sword.
(Judg 3:16)

réxev
N: chariot(s) (m)
The water returned and covered the
chariots. (Exod 14:28)

נִלְחַם \ יִלָּחֵם

דָּוִד נִלְחָם בְּגָלְיָת

לחם | וַיִּלָּחֶם | הִלָּחֵם | הַלָּחֵם

הָרַג \ יַהֲרֹג

שִׁמְעוֹן וְלֵוִי הֹרְגִים אֶת־חֲמוֹר וּבְנוֹ

הרג | וַיַּהֲרֹג | הָרֹג | הָרֹג

הִכָּה \ יַכֶּה

מֹשֶׁה מַכֶּה בַצּוּר

נכה | וַיַּךְ | הַךְ\הַכֶּה | הַכּוֹת

יָרַשׁ \ יִירַשׁ

בְּנֵי־יִשְׂרָאֵל יֹרְשִׁים אֶת־כְּנַעַן

ירש | וַיִּירַשׁ | רֵשׁ | רֶשֶׁת

---

nilxám / yilaxém
NI: fight
David is fighting Goliath.
(1 Sam 17:10)

hiká / yaké
HI: hit, strike
Moses is striking the rock.
(Exod 17:6)

harág / yaharóg
Q: slay (usually with a sword)
Simeon and Levi are slaying Hamor
and his son. (Gen 34:26)

yarásh / yirásh
Q: take possession of
The children of Israel are taking
possession of Canaan. (Josh 12:1)

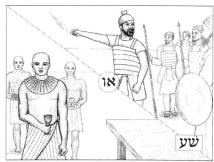

צָבָא \ צְבָאוֹת

וְנַעֲמָן שַׂר־צְבָא מֶלֶךְ־אֲרָם

שַׂר \ שָׂרִים

וַיְשִׂמֵהוּ שַׂר־אֶלֶף

גִּבּוֹר \ גִּבּוֹרִים

וַיִּשְׁלַח אֵת כָּל־הַצָּבָא הַגִּבֹּרִים

אֹיֵב \ אֹיְבִים

אִישׁ צַר וְאוֹיֵב הָמָן הָרָע הַזֶּה

---

tsavá / tsəva'ót
N: army, host (m)
Naaman was the commander of the
army of the king of Syria. (2 Kgs 5:1)

sár / sarím
N: commander; chief official (m)
He set him as a commander of a
thousand. (1 Sam 18:13)

gibór / giborím
N: warrior, mighty man (m)
And he sent all the army, that is, the
mighty men. (2 Sam 10:7)

oyév / oyvím
N: enemy (m)
"A foe and an enemy is this evil
Haman." (Esth 7:6)

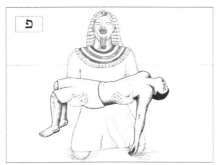

מֵת \ יָמוּת

בְּכוֹר פַּרְעֹה מֵת

מוּת | וַיָּ֫מָת | מוּת | מוּת

אָבַד \ יֹאבַד

הָאֲתֹנוֹת לַאֲבִי שָׁאוּל אֹבְדוֹת

אבד | וַיֹּאבַד | — | אֲבַד

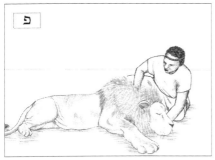

הֵמִית \ יָמִית

דָּוִד מֵמִית אֶת־הָאֲרִי

מוּת | וַיָּ֫מֶת | הֵמֵת | הֵמִית

קָבַר \ יִקְבֹּר

בְּנֵי יַעֲקֹב קֹבְרִים אֹתוֹ בִּמְעָרָה

קבר | וַיִּקְבֹּר | קֹבֵר | קָבַר

mét / yamút
Q: die
The firstborn of Pharaoh is dying.
(Exod 11:5)

avád / yovád
Q: become lost, perish
The donkeys that belong to the
father of Saul are lost. (1 Sam 9:3)

hemít / yamít
HI: kill
David is killing the lion.
(1 Sam 17:35)

qavár / yiqbór
Q: bury
Jacob's sons are burying him in a
cave. (Gen 50:13)

3.6
Education

חָשַׁב \ יַחְשֹׁב

עֵלִי חֹשֵׁב אֶת־חַנָּה לְשִׁכֹּרָה

חשב | וַיַּחְשֹׁב | — | חָשַׁב

יָדַע \ יֵדַע

נֹחַ יֵדַע כִּי־קַלּוּ הַמַּיִם מֵעַל הָאָרֶץ

ידע | וַיֵּדַע | דַּע | דֹּעַת

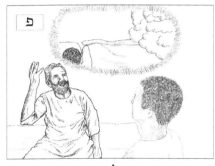

בָּן \ יָבִין

עֵלִי בָּן כִּי יְהוָה קֹרֵא לַנַּעַר

בין | וַיָּבֶן | בִּין | —

הֵבִין \ יָבִין

גַּבְרִיאֵל מֵבִין לוֹ אֶת־הַמַּרְאֶה

בין | וַיָּבֶן | הָבֵן | הָבִין

---

xasháv / yaxshóv
Q: think
Eli thinks Hannah is a drunken
woman. (1 Sam 1:13)

bán / yavín
Q: perceive, understand
Eli perceives that YHWH is calling
the young man. (1 Sam 3:8)

yadá / yedá
Q: know
Noah knows that the waters became
light from upon the earth. (Gen 8:11)

hevín / yavín
HI: explain; understand
Gabriel is explaining to him the
vision. (Dan 8:16)

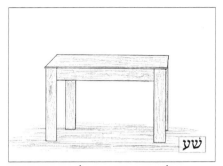

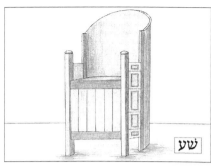

שֻׁלְחָן \ שֻׁלְחָנוֹת

וְשַׂמְתָּ אֶת־הַשֻּׁלְחָן מִחוּץ לַפָּרֹכֶת

כִּסֵּא \ כִּסְאוֹת

וְנָשִׂים לוֹ שָׁם מִטָּה וְשֻׁלְחָן וְכִסֵּא

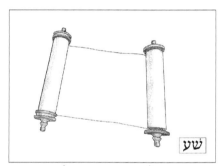

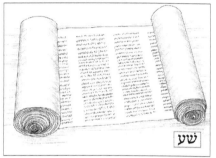

מְגִלָּה \ מְגִלּוֹת

אַחֲרֵי שְׂרֹף הַמֶּלֶךְ אֶת־הַמְּגִלָּה

סֵפֶר \ סְפָרִים

זֶה סֵפֶר תּוֹלְדֹת אָדָם

---

shulxán / shulxanót
N: table (m)
"And you shall place the table
outside the curtain." (Exod 26:35)

kisé / kis'ót
N: chair, throne (m)
"And let us set for him there a bed
and a table and a chair." (2 Kgs 4:10)

məgilá / məgilót
N: scroll (f)
... after the king burned the scroll.
(Jer 36:27)

séfer / sfarím
N: document, writing (m)
This is the document of the
generations of Adam. (Gen 5:1)

דִּבֶּר \ יְדַבֵּר

שָׁמַע \ יִשְׁמַע

פַּרְעֹה מְדַבֵּר אֶל־מֹשֶׁה וְאַהֲרֹן

גִּדְעוֹן שֹׁמֵעַ אֶת־מִסְפֵּר הַחֲלוֹם

דבר | וַיְדַבֵּר | דִּבֶּר | דִּבֶּר

שמע | וַיִּשְׁמַע | שֹׁמֵעַ | שָׁמֹעַ

כָּתַב \ יִכְתֹּב

קָרָא \ יִקְרָא

בָּרוּךְ כֹּתֵב אֶת־דִּבְרֵי יְהוָה

אֵשֶׁת־פּוֹטִיפַר קֹרֵאת לָאֲנָשִׁים

כתב | וַיִּכְתֹּב | כָּתַב | כְּתֹב

קרא | וַיִּקְרָא | קֹרֵא | קְרֹא

---

dibér / yədabér
PI: speak
Pharaoh is speaking to Moses and
Aaron. (Exod 7:9)

shamá / yishmá
Q: hear; obey
Gideon is hearing the telling of the
dream. (Judg 7:15)

katáv / yixtóv
Q: write
Baruch is writing the words of
YHWH. (Jer 36:4)

qará / yiqrá
Q: call out; read (aloud)
The wife of Potiphar is calling out to
the men. (Gen 39:14)

4
The Constructed Order

4.1
Building and Travel

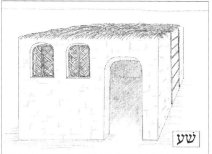

עִיר \ עָרִים

לֵךְ אֶל־נִינְוֵה הָעִיר הַגְּדוֹלָה

בַּיִת \ בָּתִּים

אֵינֶנּוּ גָדוֹל בַּבַּיִת הַזֶּה מִמֶּנִּי

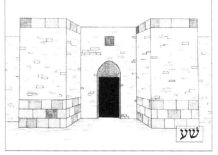

חוֹמָה \ חוֹמוֹת

וּבַחוֹמָה הִיא יוֹשָׁבֶת

שַׁעַר \ שְׁעָרִים

וְיִרַשׁ זַרְעֲךָ אֵת שַׁעַר אֹיְבָיו

ír / arím
N: city, town (f)
"Walk to Nineveh, the great city."
(Jon 1:2)

báyt / batím
N: house (m)
"There is no one greater in this
house than me." (Gen 39:9)

xomá / xomót
N: wall (of a city, typically) (f)
And in the city wall she was
dwelling. (Josh 2:15)

shá'ar / shə'arím
N: gate (m)
"And your seed shall possess the
gate of his enemies." (Gen 22:17)

חֶ֫דֶר \ חֲדָרִים

וַיָּבֹא הַחַ֫דְרָה וַיֵּבְךְ שָׁ֫מָּה

קִיר \ קִירוֹת

וְהִנֵּה הַנֶּ֫גַע בְּקִירֹת הַבַּ֫יִת

דֶּ֫לֶת \ דְּלָתוֹת

וַיֵּצֵא לוֹט וְהַדֶּ֫לֶת סָגַר אַחֲרָיו

חַלּוֹן \ חַלּוֹנוֹת

וַתֹּ֫רֶד מִיכַל אֶת־דָּוִד בְּעַד הַחַלּוֹן

---

xéder / xadarím
N: room, chamber (m)
He entered into the room and wept
there. (Gen 43:30)

qír / qirót
N: wall (of a house, typically) (m)
And behold the disease was in the
walls of the house. (Lev 14:37)

délet / dəlatót
N: door (f)
Lot went out, and he shut the door
behind him. (Gen 19:6)

xalón / xalonót
N: window (f)
And Michal lowered David through
the window. (1 Sam 19:12)

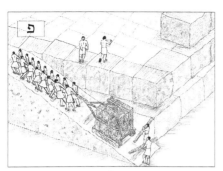

בָּנָה \ יִבְנֶה

בְּנֵי הָאָדָם בֹּנִים מִגְדָּל

בנה | וַיִּבֶן | בֹּנֶה | בָּנוֹת

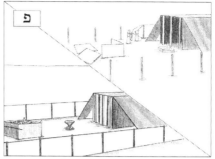

כָּלָה \ יִכְלֶה

*כָּל־עֲבֹדַת הַמִּשְׁכָּן כָּלְתָה

כלה | וַיְכַל | — | כְּלוֹת

עָבַד \ יַעֲבֹד

יַעֲקֹב עָבַד בְּרָחֵל שֶׁבַע שָׁנִים

עבד | וַיַּעֲבֹד | עֹבֵד | עֲבֹד

נָח \ יָנוּחַ

הַתֵּבָה נָחָה עַל הָרֵי אֲרָרָט

נוח | וַיָּנַח | נוֹחַ | נוֹחַ

---

baná / yivné
Q: build
The children of man are building a tower. (Gen 11:4)

avád / ya'avód
Q: work, serve
Jacob is working seven years for Rachel. (Gen 29:20)

kalá / yixlé
Q: be finished
All the work of the tabernacle was finished. (Exod 39:32)

náx / yanúax
Q: rest
The ark is resting on the mountains of Ararat. (Gen 8:4)

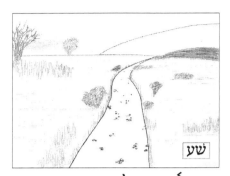

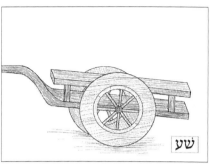

דֶּ֫רֶךְ \ דְּרָכִים

עֲגָלָה \ עֲגָלוֹת

וַיַּרְא אֶת־מַלְאַךְ יְהוָה נִצָּב בַּדֶּ֫רֶךְ

וַיָּשִׂ֫מוּ אֶת־הָאָרוֹן אֶל־הָעֲגָלָה

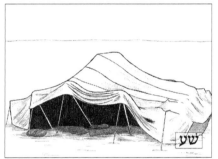

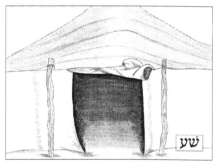

אֹ֫הֶל \ אֱהָלִים

פֶּ֫תַח \ פְּתָחִים

וַיָּבֹא לָבָן בְּאֹ֫הֶל יַעֲקֹב

וְהוּא יֹשֵׁב פֶּ֫תַח־הָאֹ֫הֶל

---

dérex / draxím
N: path, way (f)
And he saw the angel of YHWH standing in the path. (Num 22:31)

ohel / ohalím
N: tent (m)
And Laban entered into the tent of Jacob. (Gen 31:33)

agalá / agalót
N: wagon, cart (f)
And they placed the ark on the cart. (1 Sam 6:11)

pétax / pətaxím
N: opening (m)
And he was sitting at the opening of the tent. (Gen 18:1)

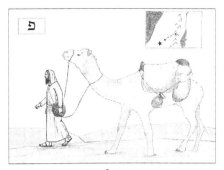

נָסַע \ יִסַּע

אַבְרָהָם נֹסֵעַ אַרְצָה הַנֶּגֶב

נסע | וַיִּסַּע | סַע | נְסֹעַ

הִתְהַלֵּךְ \ יִתְהַלֵּךְ

אַבְרָם מִתְהַלֵּךְ בְּאֶרֶץ־כְּנָעַן

הלך | וַיִּתְהַלֵּךְ | הִתְהַלֵּךְ | הִתְהַלֵּךְ

חָנָה \ יַחֲנֶה

בְּנֵי יִשְׂרָאֵל חֹנִים עַל־הַיָּם

חנה | וַיִּחַן | חָנָה | חֲנוֹת

שָׁכַן \ יִשְׁכֹּן

אַבְרָם שֹׁכֵן בְּאֵלֹנֵי מַמְרֵא

שכן | וַיִּשְׁכֹּן | שְׁכֹן | שָׁכַן

---

nasá / yisá
Q: journey, depart
Abraham is journeying to the land
of the Negev. (Gen 20:1)

xaná / yaxané
Q: set up camp, encamp
The children of Israel are encamping
by the sea. (Exod 14:9)

hithaléx / yithaléx
HTP: walk about
Abram is walking about in the land
of Canaan. (Gen 13:17)

shaxán / yishkón
Q: dwell
Abram is dwelling among the oaks
of Mamre. (Gen 14:13)

4.2
Measurement and Numbers

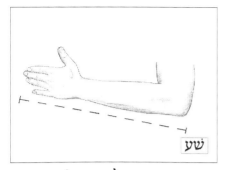

אַמָּה \ אַמּוֹת

גָּבְהוֹ שֵׁשׁ אַמּוֹת וָזָרֶת

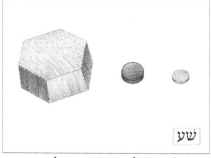

שֶׁקֶל \ שְׁקָלִים

שְׂעַר רֹאשׁוֹ מָאתַיִם שְׁקָלִים

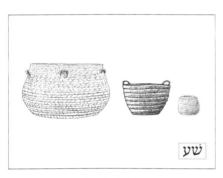

אֵיפָה

גְּדִי־עִזִּים וְאֵיפַת־קֶמַח מַצּוֹת

הִין

יַיִן תַּקְרִיב לַנֶּסֶךְ חֲצִי הַהִין

---

amá / amót
N: cubit (~18 inches) (f)
His height was six cubits and a
span. (1 Sam 17:4)

shéqel / shqalím
N: shekel (~.4 ounces) (m)
The hair of his head was 200
shekels. (2 Sam 14:26)

efá
N: ephah (~20 dry quarts) (f)
... a young goat and an ephah of flour
for unleavened bread. (Judg 6:19)

hín
N: hin (~1 gallon) (f)
"Bring near wine for the drink
offering, half of the hin." (Num 15:10)

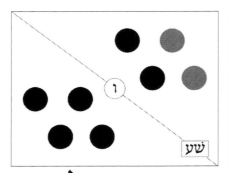

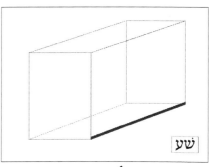

חֲצִי · כֹּל

בַּחֲצִי הַלַּיְלָה וַיַּךְ כָּל־בְּכוֹר

אֹרֶךְ

וְעָשִׂיתָ שֻׁלְחָן אַמָּתַיִם אָרְכּוֹ

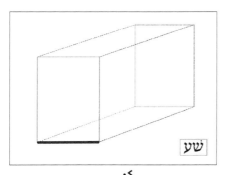

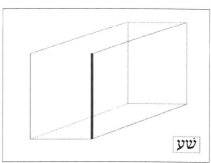

רֹחַב

וְאַמָּה רָחְבּוֹ

קוֹמָה

וְאַמָּה וָחֵצִי קֹמָתוֹ

---

xatsí / kól N: half, middle; all, each, every In the middle of the night, he struck every firstborn. (Exod 12:29)	*órex* N: length "And you shall make a table, two cubits its length ..." (Exod 25:23)
róxav N: width "... and a cubit its width ..." (Exod 25:23)	*qomá* N: height "... and a cubit and a half its height." (Exod 25:23)

כָּבֵד \ כְּבֵדָה

כִּי־כָבֵד מִמְּךָ הַדָּבָר

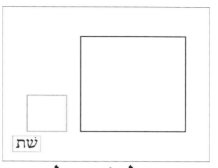

גָּדוֹל \ גְּדוֹלָה

הַמָּאוֹר הַגָּדֹל לְמֶמְשֶׁלֶת הַיּוֹם

רַב \ רַבָּה

וַנֵּשֶׁב בְּמִצְרַיִם יָמִים רַבִּים

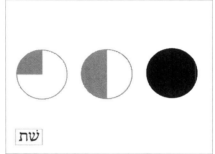

שָׁלֵם \ שְׁלֵמָה

הִתְהַלַּכְתִּי לְפָנֶיךָ בְּלֵבָב שָׁלֵם

---

kavéd / kəvedá
ADJ: heavy; honored (m/f)
"... because the thing is too heavy
for you." (Exod 18:18)

gadól / gədolá
ADJ: big, great (m/f)
... the great light for ruling the day.
(Gen 1:16)

ráv / rabá
ADJ: much, many; great (m/f)
"And we dwelt in Egypt many days."
(Num 20:15)

shalém / shlemá
ADJ: whole, complete (m/f)
"I have walked before you with a
whole heart." (2 Kgs 20:3)

רִאשׁוֹן \ רִאשֹׁנָה

זֶה יָצָא רִאשֹׁנָה

שֵׁנִי \ שֵׁנִית

וַיִּישַׁן וַיַּחֲלֹם שֵׁנִית

שְׁלִישִׁי \ שְׁלִישִׁית

וַיְצַו אֶת־הַשֵּׁנִי וְאֶת־הַשְּׁלִישִׁי

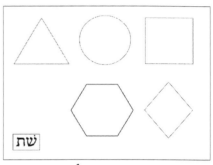

אַחֵר \ אַחֶרֶת

וְהִנֵּה שֶׁבַע פָּרוֹת אֲחֵרוֹת עֹלוֹת

---

rishón / rishoná
ADJ: first (m/f)
"This one came out first."
(Gen 38:28)

shlishí / shlishít
ADJ: third (m/f)
He commanded the second man and
the third man. (Gen 32:20*)

shení / shenít
ADJ: second (m/f)
He fell asleep and dreamed a second
time. (Gen 41:5)

axér / axéret
ADJ: other, another (m/f)
And, behold, seven other cows were
coming up. (Gen 41:3)

יָסַף \ יֹסֵף

מֹשֶׁה יֹסֵף עוֹד שָׁלֹשׁ עָרִים

יסף | — | סֹף | —

סָפַר \ יִסְפֹּר

אַבְרָם סָפַר אֶת־הַכּוֹכָבִים

ספר | וַיִּסְפֹּר | סָפַר | סָפֹר

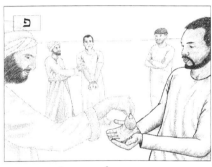

מָכַר \ יִמְכֹּר

אֲחֵי יוֹסֵף מֹכְרִים אֹתוֹ

מכר | וַיִּמְכֹּר | מָכֹר | מָכַר

קָנָה \ יִקְנֶה

פּוֹטִיפַר קָנָה אֶת־יוֹסֵף

קנה | וַיִּקֶן | קָנָה | קָנוֹת

---

yasáf
Q: add, do again
Moses is adding another three cities.
(Deut 19:9)

safár / yispór
Q: count
Abram is counting the stars.
(Gen 15:5)

maxár / yimkór
Q: sell
Joseph's brothers are selling him.
(Gen 37:28)

qaná / yiqné
Q: buy, acquire
Potiphar is buying Joseph.
(Gen 39:1)

9
276
14
שׁע

שׁת
1

מִסְפָּר
אֲבָנִים כְּמִסְפַּר שִׁבְטֵי יִשְׂרָאֵל

אֶחָד \ אַחַת
וַיְהִי כָל־הָאָרֶץ שָׂפָה אַחַת

2
שׁע

3
שׁע

שְׁנַיִם \ שְׁתַּיִם
שְׁנַיִם מִכֹּל תָּבִיא אֶל־הַתֵּבָה

שְׁלֹשָׁה \ שָׁלוֹשׁ
וַיַּרְא וְהִנֵּה שְׁלֹשָׁה אֲנָשִׁים

---

mispár
N: number (m)
... stones according to the number
of the tribes of Israel. (1 Kgs 18:31)

exád / axát
ADJ: one (m/f)
All of the earth was one language.
(Gen 11:1)

shnáym / shtáym
N: two (m/f)
"Two of everything you shall bring
to the ark." (Gen 6:19)

shloshá / shalósh
N: three (m/f)
He looked, and behold, there were
three men. (Gen 18:2)

4 שע	5 שע

אַרְבָּעָה \ אַרְבַּע

וְעָשִׂיתָ קַרְנֹתָיו עַל אַרְבַּע פִּנֹּתָיו

חֲמִשָּׁה \ חָמֵשׁ

וַיָּנֻסוּ חֲמֵשֶׁת הַמְּלָכִים הָאֵלֶּה

6 שע	7 שע

שִׁשָּׁה \ שֵׁשׁ

יָלַדְתִּי לוֹ שִׁשָּׁה בָנִים

שִׁבְעָה \ שֶׁבַע

שֶׁבַע פָּרֹת שֶׁבַע שָׁנִים הֵנָּה

---

arba'á / arbá
N: four (m/f)
"And you shall make its horns on its
four corners." (Exod 27:2)

shishá / shésh
N: six (m/f)
"I have borne for him six sons."
(Gen 30:20)

xamishá / xamésh
N: five (m/f)
And these five kings fled.
(Josh 10:16)

shiv'á / shéva
N: seven (m/f)
"Seven cows are seven years."
(Gen 41:26)

8 | שע

שְׁמֹנֶה \ שְׁמֹנָה

וַיָּמָל אֶת־יִצְחָק בֶּן־שְׁמֹנַת יָמִים

9 | שע

תֵּשַׁע \ תִּשְׁעָה

לְתִשְׁעַת הַמַּטּוֹת וַחֲצִי הַמַּטֶּה

10 | שע

עֶשֶׂר \ עֲשָׂרָה

אוּלַי יִמָּצְאוּן שָׁם עֲשָׂרָה

11 12 13
14 15 16
17 18 19 | שע

־עָשָׂרֵה \ ־עָשָׂר

שְׁתֵּי עֶשְׂרֵה שָׁנָה שְׁנֵי־עָשָׂר חֹדֶשׁ

---

shmoná / shmoné
N: eight (m/f)
And he circumcised Isaac at eight
days old. (Gen 21:4)

tish'á / tésha
N: nine (m/f)
... to the nine tribes and the half
tribe. (Num 34:13)

asará / éser
N: ten (m/f)
"Perhaps ten are found there."
(Gen 18:32)

asár / esré
N: -teen (m/f)
... the twelfth year, the twelfth
month. (Ezek 32:1)

20 שע	50 שע
עֶשְׂרִים	חֲמִשִּׁים
שָׁפַט אֶת־יִשְׂרָאֵל עֶשְׂרִים שָׁנָה	אוּלַי יֵשׁ חֲמִשִּׁים צַדִּיקִם בָּעִיר

100 שע	1000 שע
מֵאָה \ מֵאוֹת	אֶלֶף \ אֲלָפִים
וְאַבְרָהָם בֶּן־מְאַת שָׁנָה	הִנֵּה נָתַתִּי אֶלֶף כֶּסֶף לְאָחִיךְ

---

esrím
N: twenty
He judged Israel for twenty years.
(Judg 16:31)

me'á / me'ót
N: hundred (f)
And Abraham was one hundred
years old. (Gen 21:5)

xamishím
N: fifty
"Perhaps there are fifty righteous
people in the city." (Gen 18:24)

élef / alafím
N: thousand (m)
"Behold, I give a thousand (pieces of)
silver to your brother." (Gen 20:16)

5
Word Groups

5.1
Movement Verbs

יָצָא \ יֵצֵא

בַּת־יִפְתָּח יֹצֵאת לִקְרָאתוֹ

יצא | וַיֵּצֵא | צֵא | צֵאת

בָּא \ יָבוֹא

שְׁנַיִם שְׁנַיִם הֵם בָּאִים אֶל־נֹחַ

בוא | וַיָּבֹא | בֹּא | בָּא

סָר \ יָסוּר

מֹשֶׁה סָר לִרְאוֹת אֶת־הַסְּנֶה

סור | וַיָּסַר | סוּר | סָר

שָׁב \ יָשׁוּב

הַיּוֹנָה שָׁבָה אֶל־הַתֵּבָה

שוב | וַיָּשָׁב | שׁוּב | שׁוּב

---

yatsá / yetsé
Q: go out
Jepthah's daughter is going out to
meet him. (Judg 11:34)

sár / yasúr
Q: turn aside
Moses is turning aside to see the
bush. (Exod 3:3)

bá / yavó
Q: come, enter
Two by two they are coming to
Noah. (Gen 7:9)

sháv / yashúv
Q: return
The dove is returning to the ark.
(Gen 8:9)

יָשַׁב \ יֵשֵׁב

יוֹנָה יָשַׁב תַּחַת הַסֻּכָּה

ישב | וַיֵּשֶׁב | שֵׁב | שֶׁבֶת

קָם \ יָקוּם

שְׁמוּאֵל קָם לָלֶכֶת אֶל־עֵלִי

קום | וַיָּקָם | קוּם | קוּם

שָׁכַב \ יִשְׁכַּב

יַעֲקֹב שָׁכַב עַל־אֶבֶן

שכב | וַיִּשְׁכַּב | שְׁכַב | שָׁכַב

עָמַד \ יַעֲמֹד

מֹשֶׁה עָמַד עַל־אַדְמַת קֹדֶשׁ

עמד | וַיַּעֲמֹד | עֲמֹד | עָמַד

---

yasháv / yeshév
Q: sit; dwell
Jonah is sitting under the shelter.
(Jon 4:5)

qám / yaqúm
Q: arise, get up
Samuel is getting up to walk to Eli.
(1 Sam 3:6)

shaxáv / yishkáv
Q: lie down
Jacob is lying down on a rock.
(Gen 28:11)

amád / ya'amód
Q: stand
Moses is standing on holy ground.
(Exod 3:5)

עָלָה \ יַעֲלֶה

מֹשֶׁה עָלָה אֶל־רֹאשׁ הָהָר

עלה | וַיַּעַל | עָלָה | עֲלוֹת

יָרַד \ יֵרֵד

יוֹנָה יָרַד אֶל־יַרְכְּתֵי הַסְּפִינָה

ירד | וַיֵּרֶד | רֵד | רֶדֶת

הָלַךְ \ יֵלֵךְ

אַבְרָהָם וְיִצְחָק הֹלְכִים אֶל־הָהָר

הלך | וַיֵּלֶךְ | לֵךְ | לֶכֶת

רָץ \ יָרוּץ

אֲחִימַעַץ רָץ אֶל־דָּוִד

רוץ | וַיָּרָץ | רוּץ | רוּץ

---

alá / ya'alé
Q: go up
Moses is going up to the top of the
mountain. (Exod 19:20)

yarád / yeréd
Q: go down
Jonah is going down into the rear
parts of the ship. (Jon 1:5)

haláx / yeléx
Q: walk, go
Abraham and Isaac are walking to
the mountain. (Gen 22:8)

ráts / yarúts
Q: run
Ahimaaz is running to David.
(2 Sam 18:19)

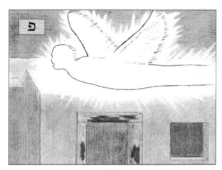

עָבַר \ יַעֲבֹר

מַלְאַךְ יְהוָה עֹבֵר בְּאֶרֶץ־מִצְרָיִם

עבר | וַיַּעֲבֹר | עֹבֵר | עֲבֹר

סָבַב \ יָסֹב

כָּל הָאֲנָשִׁים סֹבְבִים אֶת־הָעִיר

סבב | וַיִּסֹּב | סֹב | סָבַב

פָּנָה \ יִפְנֶה

פַּרְעֹה פָּנָה מֵעִם מֹשֶׁה וְאַהֲרֹן

פנה | וַיִּפֶן | פָּנֶה | פָּנוֹת

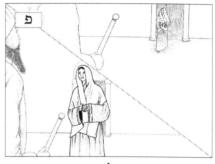

קָרַב \ יִקְרַב

אֶסְתֵּר קֹרֶבֶת אֶל־הַמֶּלֶךְ

קרב | וַיִּקְרַב | קָרַב | קֹרֵב

---

avár / ya'avór
Q: pass over, pass by
The angel of YHWH is passing over
the land of Egypt. (Exod 12:12)

paná / yifné
Q: turn
Pharaoh is turning away from
Moses and Aaron. (Exod 7:23)

saváv / yasóv
Q: go around
All of the men are going around
the city. (Josh 6:3)

qaráv / yiqráv
Q: come near
Esther is coming near to the king.
(Esth 5:2)

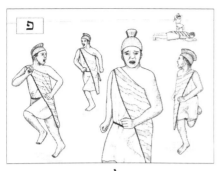

נָס \ יָנוּס

הַפְּלִשְׁתִּים נָסִים מִפְּנֵי דָוִד

נוס | וַיָּנָס | נוּס | נוּס

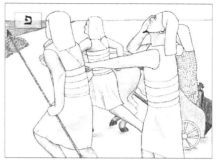

רָדַף \ יִרְדֹּף

מִצְרַיִם רֹדְפִים אַחֲרֵי בְּנֵי יִשְׂרָאֵל

רדף | וַיִּרְדֹּף | רְדֹף | רָדַף

גָּלָה \ יִגְלֶה

יִשְׂרָאֵל גָּלָה מֵעַל אַדְמָתוֹ אַשּׁוּרָה

גלה | וַיִּגֶל | גְּלֵה | גָּלוֹת

נִשְׁאַר \ יִשָּׁאֵר

נָעֳמִי נִשְׁאֶרֶת מִיַּלְדֶיהָ וּמֵאִישָׁהּ

שאר | וַיִּשָּׁאֵר | — | —

---

nás / yanús
Q: flee
The Philistines are fleeing before
David. (1 Sam 17:51)

radáf / yirdóf
Q: pursue, chase
Egypt is chasing after the children
of Israel. (Exod 14:9)

galá / yiglé
Q: depart (into exile)
Israel is going into exile from its
ground to Assyria. (2 Kgs 17:23)

nish'ár / yisha'ér
NI: remain, be left over
Naomi is left without her boys and
without her husband. (Ruth 1:5)

5.2
Action and Stative Verbs

לָקַח \ יִקַּח

שִׁמְשׁוֹן לֹקֵחַ לְחִי־חֲמוֹר טְרִיָּה

לקח | וַיִּקַּח | קַח | לָּחַת

נָתַן \ יִתֵּן

חַוָּה נֹתֶנֶת אֶת־הַפְּרִי לְאִישָׁהּ

נתן | וַיִּתֵּן | תֵּן | תֵּת

נָשָׂא \ יִשָּׂא

בְּנֵי־יִשְׂרָאֵל נֹשְׂאִים אֲבָנִים

נשׂא | וַיִּשָּׂא | שָׂא | שְׂאֵת\נְשׂא

שָׂם \ יָשִׂים

אַבְרָהָם שָׂם אֹתוֹ עַל־הַמִּזְבֵּחַ

שׂים | וַיָּשֶׂם | שִׂים | שִׂים

---

laqáx / yiqáx
Q: take, grab
Samson is taking a fresh jawbone of a donkey. (Judg 15:15)

natán / yitén
Q: give
Eve is giving the fruit to her husband. (Gen 3:6)

nasá / yisá
Q: pick up; carry
The children of Israel are picking up stones. (Josh 4:8)

sám / yasím
Q: set down, place
Abraham is placing him on the altar. (Gen 22:9)

לָכַד \ יִלְכֹּד

שִׁמְשׁוֹן לֹכֵד שׁוּעָל

לכד | וַיִּלְכֹּד | לְכֹד | לָכַד

הִשְׁלִיךְ \ יַשְׁלִיךְ

אַהֲרֹן מַשְׁלִיךְ מַטֵּהוּ לִפְנֵי פַרְעֹה

שׁלד | וַיַּשְׁלֵךְ | הַשְׁלֵךְ | הִשְׁלִיךְ

בָּחַר \ יִבְחַר

דָּוִד בֹּחֵר לוֹ חָמֵשׁ אֲבָנִים

בחר | וַיִּבְחַר | בְּחַר | בָּחַר

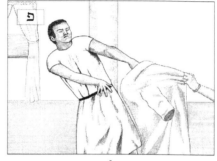

עָזַב \ יַעֲזֹב

יוֹסֵף עֹזֵב בִּגְדוֹ בְּיַד־אֵשֶׁת אֲדֹנָיו

עזב | וַיַּעֲזֹב | עֲזֹב | עָזַב

---

laxád / yilkód
Q: seize, catch
Samson is seizing a fox.
(Judg 15:4)

hishlíx / yashlíx
HI: throw
Aaron is throwing his staff before
Pharaoh. (Exod 7:10)

baxár / yivxár
Q: choose
David is choosing for himself five
stones. (1 Sam 17:40)

azáv / ya'azóv
Q: leave, forsake
Joseph is leaving his garment in the
hand of his master's wife. (Gen 39:12)

פ

פ

פָּתַח \ יִפְתַּח

סָגַר \ יִסְגֹּר

נֹחַ פָּתַח אֶת־חַלּוֹן הַתֵּבָה

הַמַּלְאָכִים סֹגְרִים אֶת־דֶּלֶת הַבַּיִת

פתח | וַיִּפְתַּח | פָּתַח | פָּתַח

סגר | וַיִּסְגֹּר | סָגַר | סָגַר

פ

פ

אָסַף \ יֶאֱסֹף

שָׁפַךְ \ יִשְׁפֹּךְ

הָעָם אֹסְפִים אֶת־הַשְּׂלָו

מֹשֶׁה שָׁפַךְ מַיִם עַל־הַיַּבָּשָׁה

אסף | וַיֶּאֱסֹף | אָסֹף | אָסֹף

שפך | וַיִּשְׁפֹּךְ | שָׁפַךְ | שָׁפַךְ

patáx / yiftáx
Q: open
Noah is opening the window of the
ark. (Gen 8:6)

sagár / yisgór
Q: close
The angels are shutting the door of
the house. (Gen 19:10)

asáf / ye'esóf
Q: gather
The people are gathering the quail.
(Num 11:32)

shafáx / yishpóx
Q: pour out
Moses is pouring water onto the dry
ground. (Exod 4:9)

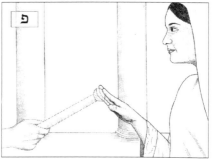

נָגַע \ יִגַּע

אֶסְתֵּר נֹגַעַת בְּרֹאשׁ הַשַּׁרְבִיט

נגע | וַיִּגַּע | גַּע | נֹגֵעַ/גַּעַת

רָאָה \ יִרְאֶה

חַוָּה רֹאָה כִּי טוֹב הָעֵץ לְמַאֲכָל

ראה | וַיַּרְא | רְאֵה | רְאוֹת

כִּלָּה \ יְכַלֶּה

בְּנֵי יַעֲקֹב מְכַלִּים אֶת־הַשֶּׁבֶר

כלה | וַיְכַל | כַּלֵּה | כַּלּוֹת

הֵחֵל \ יָחֵל

מִצְרִי מֵחֵל בַּגָּדוֹל

חלל | וַיָּחֶל | הָחֵל | הָחֵל

---

ra'á / yir'é
Q: see
Eve sees that the tree is good for food. (Gen 3:6)

hexél / yaxél
HI: begin
An Egyptian is beginning with the oldest. (Gen 44:12)

nagá / yigá
Q: touch
Esther is touching the head of the scepter. (Esth 5:2)

kilá / yəxalé
PI: complete, finish
The sons of Jacob are finishing the grain. (Gen 43:2)

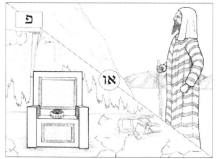

נָפַל \ יִפֹּל

דָּגוֹן נֹפֵל לִפְנֵי אֲרוֹן יְהוָה

נפל | וַיִּפֹּל | נָפַל | נָפֹל

נָכוֹן \ יִכּוֹן

מֹשֶׁה נָכוֹן לַעֲלֹת אֶל־הַר סִינַי

כון | וַיִּכּוֹן | הֻכּוֹן | —

מָלֵא \ יִמְלָא

הַכְּלִי מָלֵא שֶׁמֶן

מלא | וַיִּמְלָא | מָלָא | מְלֹאת

חָסֵר \ יֶחְסַר

*צַפַּחַת הַשֶּׁמֶן חָסֵרָה

חסר | וַיֶּחְסַר | — | —

nafál / yipól
Q: fall
Dagon is falling before the ark of
YHWH. (1 Sam 5:3)

naxón / yikón
NI: be ready; be established
Moses is ready to go up to Mount
Sinai. (Exod 34:2)

malé / yimlá
Q: be full
The vessel is full of oil.
(2 Kgs 4:6)

xasér / yexsár
Q: be lacking, be empty
The jug of oil was empty.
(1 Kgs 17:14)

אָהַב \ יֶאֱהַב

יַעֲקֹב אֹהֵב אֶת־רָחֵל מִלֵּאָה

אהב | וַיֶּאֱהַב | אֱהַב | אַהֲבָה/אֹהֵב

שָׂנֵא \ יִשְׂנָא

אֲחֵי יוֹסֵף שֹׂנְאִים אֹתוֹ

שׂנא | וַיִּשְׂנָא | שְׂנָא | שֹׂנֵא

שָׂמַח \ יִשְׂמַח

יוֹנָה שָׂמֵחַ עַל־הַקִּיקָיוֹן

שׂמח | וַיִּשְׂמַח | שְׂמַח | שָׂמֵחַ

בָּכָה \ יִבְכֶּה

עֵשָׂו בֹּכֶה כִּי אֵין לְאָבִיו בְּרָכָה

בכה | וַיֵּבְךְּ | בְּכֵה | בְּכוֹת

---

aháv / ye'eháv
Q: love
Jacob loves Rachel more than Leah.
(Gen 29:30)

samáx / yismáx
Q: be glad, be happy
Jonah is happy concerning the plant.
(Jon 4:6)

sané / yisná
Q: hate
Joseph's brothers hate him.
(Gen 37:4)

baxá / yivké
Q: cry, weep
Esau is crying because his father
does not have a blessing. (Gen 27:38)

בָּטַח \ יִבְטַח

אִישׁ בֹּטֵחַ עַל־מִשְׁעֶנֶת

בטח | וַיִּבְטַח | בָּטַח | בֹּטֵחַ

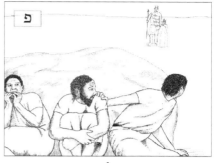

יָרֵא \ יִירָא

אַנְשֵׁי יִשְׂרָאֵל יְרֵאִים מִפְּנֵי גָלְיָת

ירא | וַיִּירָא | יָרֵא | יְרֵאָה

be able

יָכֹל \ יוּכַל

*לֹא־יוּכַל הַנַּעַר לַעֲזֹב אֶת־אָבִיו

יכל | וַיֻּכַל | — | יָכֹלְתָּ

בּוֹשׁ \ יֵבוֹשׁ

הַבֹּטֵחַ בַּפֶּסֶל בּוֹשׁ

בוש | וַיֵּבוֹשׁ | בּוֹשׁ | בּוֹשׁ

---

batáx / yivtáx
Q: trust, rely
A man is trusting in a staff.
(2 Kgs 18:21)

yaxól / yuxál
Q: be able
The young man is not able to leave
his father. (Gen 44:22)

yaré / yirá
Q: fear
The people of Israel are fearing
before Goliath. (1 Sam 17:24)

bósh / yevósh
Q: be ashamed
The one who trusts in the idol is
ashamed. (Isa 42:17)

5.3
Derived Binyanim

נִרְאָה \ יֵרָאֶה

הַקֶּשֶׁת נִרְאָה בֶּעָנָן

ראה | וַיֵּרָא | הֵרָאָה | הֵרָאוֹת

נִמְצָא \ יִמָּצֵא

הַגָּבִיעַ נִמְצָא בְּאַמְתַּחַת בִּנְיָמִן

מצא | וַיִּמָּצֵא | — | הִמָּצֵא

הִתְחַזֵּק \ יִתְחַזֵּק

דָּוִד מִתְחַזֵּק בַּיהוָה אֱלֹהָיו

חזק | וַיִּתְחַזֵּק | הִתְחַזֵּק | הִתְחַזֵּק

הִתְהַלֵּל \ יִתְהַלֵּל

אִישׁ מִתְהַלֵּל בְּחָכְמָתוֹ וּבִגְבוּרָתוֹ

הלל | וַיִּתְהַלֵּל | הִתְהַלֵּל | הִתְהַלֵּל

---

nimtsá / yimatsé
NI: be found
The cup is found in the sack of
Benjamin. (Gen 44:12)

hithalél / yithalél
HTP: boast (praise oneself)
A man is boasting in his wisdom
and in his strength. (Jer 9:22*)

nir'á / yera'é
NI: appear
The rainbow appears in the clouds.
(Gen 9:14)

hitxazéq / yitxazéq
HTP: strengthen oneself
David is strengthening himself in
YHWH his God. (1 Sam 30:6)

חָזַק \ יְחַזֵּק

יְהוָה מְחַזֵּק אֶת־שִׁמְשׁוֹן

חזק | וַיְחַזֵּק | חִזֵּק | חַזֵּק

קִדַּשׁ \ יְקַדֵּשׁ

מֹשֶׁה מְקַדֵּשׁ אֶת־אַהֲרֹן לַיהוָה

קדש | וַיְקַדֵּשׁ | קִדֵּשׁ | קַדֵּשׁ

מִלֵּא \ יְמַלֵּא

מִצְרִי מְמַלֵּא אֶת־הָאַמְתָּחֹת אֹכֶל

מלא | וַיְמַלֵּא | מִלֵּא | מַלֵּא

שִׁלַּם \ יְשַׁלֵּם

הָאִשָּׁה מְשַׁלֶּמֶת אֶת־נִשְׁיָהּ

שלם | — | שִׁלֵּם | שַׁלֵּם

---

xizáq / yəxazéq
PI: strengthen
YHWH is strengthening Samson.
(Judg 16:28)

qidásh / yəqadésh
PI: consecrate, make holy
Moses is consecrating Aaron to
YHWH. (Exod 40:13)

milé / yəmalé
PI: fill
An Egyptian is filling the sacks with
food. (Gen 44:1)

shilám / yəshalém
PI: (re)pay, make whole
The woman is paying her debt.
(2 Kgs 4:7)

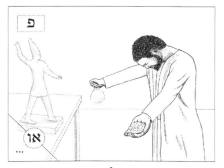

כִּבֵּד \ יְכַבֵּד

אִישׁ מְכַבֵּד אֱלוֹהַּ בְּזָהָב וּבְכֶסֶף

כבד | וַיְכַבֵּד | כִּבֵּד | כַּבֵּד

נִחַם \ יְנַחֵם

כָּל־בְּנֵי יַעֲקֹב מְנַחֲמִים אֹתוֹ

נחם | וַיְנַחֵם | נִחַם | נַחֵם

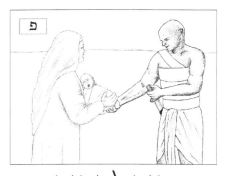

חִיָּה \ יְחַיֶּה

הַמִּצְרִי מְחַיֶּה אֶת־הַבַּת

חיה | וַיְחַיֶּה | חִיָּה | חַיּוֹת

שִׁלַּח \ יְשַׁלַּח

אִישׁ מְשַׁלֵּחַ אֶת־הַשָּׂעִיר בַּמִּדְבָּר

שלח | וַיְשַׁלַּח | שִׁלַּח | שַׁלַּח

---

kibéd / yəxabéd
PI: honor
A man is honoring a god with gold and with silver. (Dan 11:38)

nixám / yənaxém
PI: comfort
All of Jacob's sons are comforting him. (Gen 37:35)

xiyá / yəxayé
PI: let live; give life
The Egyptian is letting the daughter live. (Exod 1:22)

shiláx / yəsháláx
PI: send away
A man is sending away the goat in the wilderness. (Lev 16:22)

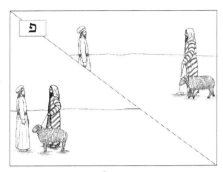

הַקְרִיב \ יַקְרִיב

מֹשֶׁה מַקְרִיב אֶת אֵיל הָעֹלָה

קרב | וַיַּקְרֵב | הַקְרֵב | הַקְרִיב

הַכְרִית \ יַכְרִית

אִישׁ מַכְרִית אֶת־הַפָּסִיל

כרת | וַיַּכְרֵת | הַכְרֵת | הַכְרִית

הַשְׁמִיעַ \ יַשְׁמִיעַ

הַמֶּלֶךְ מַשְׁמִיעַ אֶת־כָּל־יְהוּדָה

שמע | וַיַּשְׁמַע | הַשְׁמַע | הַשְׁמִיעַ

הֶחֱזִיק \ יַחֲזִיק

אֲדֹנִיָּהוּ מַחֲזִיק בְּקַרְנוֹת הַמִּזְבֵּחַ

חזק | וַיַּחֲזֵק | הַחֲזֵק | הֶחֱזִיק

---

hiqrív / yaqrív
HI: bring near
Moses is bringing near the ram of
the burnt offering. (Lev 8:18)

hishmía / yashmía
HI: proclaim (cause to hear)
The king is proclaiming to all of
Judah. (1 Kgs 15:22)

hixrít / yaxrít
HI: cut off
A man is cutting down the idol.
(Mic 5:12*)

hexezíq / yaxazíq
HI: hold tightly; strengthen
Adonijah is holding tightly to the
horns of the altar. (1 Kgs 1:50)

הֶעֱמִיד \ יַעֲמִיד

אִישׁ מַעֲמִיד אֶת־שִׁמְשׁוֹן

עמד | וַיַּעֲמֵד | הֶעֱמֵד | הַעֲמִיד

הֶעֱבִיר \ יַעֲבִיר

יַעֲקֹב מַעֲבִיר אֹתָם אֶת־הַנָּהָר

עבר | וַיַּעֲבֵר | הַעֲבֵר | הַעֲבִיר

הֵקִים \ יָקִים

אֲנָשִׁים מְקִימִים אֶת־הָעַמּוּדִים

קום | וַיָּקֶם | הָקֵם | הָקִים

הֵרִים \ יָרִים

מֹשֶׁה מֵרִים אֶת־יָדוֹ

רום | וַיָּרֶם | הָרֵם | הָרִים

---

he'emíd / ya'amíd
HI: position (cause to stand)
A man is positioning Samson.
(Judg 16:25)

heqím / yaqím
HI: raise up; establish
People are raising up the pillars.
(2 Chron 3:17)

he'evír / ya'avír
HI: send across
Jacob is sending them across the
river. (Gen 32:23)

herím / yarím
HI: lift up; exalt
Moses is lifting up his hand.
(Exod 17:11)

הֵבִיא \ יָבִיא

הָעֹרְבִים מְבִיאִים לֶחֶם לְאֵלִיָּהוּ

בוא | וַיָּבֵא | הָבֵא | הָבִיא

הֵשִׁיב \ יָשִׁיב

פְּלִשְׁתִּים מֵשִׁיבִים אֶת־הָאָרוֹן

שׁוּב | וַיָּשֶׁב | הָשֵׁב | הָשִׁיב

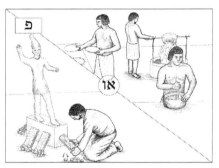

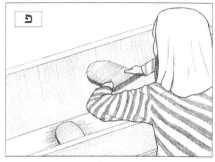

הֵכִין \ יָכִין

מִצְרִים מְכִינִים אֹכֶל לַאֲחֵי־יוֹסֵף

כון | וַיָּכֶן | הָכֵן | הָכִין

הֵנִיחַ \ יָנִיחַ

מֹשֶׁה מֵנִיחַ אֶת־הַלֻּחוֹת בָּאָרוֹן

נוח | וַיָּנַח | הַנַּח | הָנִיחַ

---

heví / yaví
HI: bring
The ravens are bringing bread to
Elijah. (1 Kgs 17:6)

hexín / yaxín
HI: prepare; make firm
Egyptians are preparing food for
Joseph's brothers. (Gen 43:16)

heshív / yashív
HI: return (someone/thing)
The Philistines are returning the
ark. (1 Sam 6:21)

heníax / yaníax
HI: cause/put to rest
Moses is laying to rest the tablets in
the ark. (1 Kgs 8:9)

הֶרְאָה \ יַרְאֶה

יָעֵל מַרְאָה בָּרָק אֶת־סִיסְרָא

ראה | וַיַּרְא | הֶרְאָה | הַרְאוֹת

הֶעֱלָה \ יַעֲלֶה

אֲחֵי יוֹסֵף מַעֲלִים אֹתוֹ מִן־הַבּוֹר

עלה | וַיַּעַל | הֵעַל | הַעֲלוֹת

הוֹצִיא \ יוֹצִיא

יְהוֹשֻׁעַ מוֹצִיא מְלָכִים מֵהַמְּעָרָה

יצא | וַיּוֹצֵא | הוֹצֵא | הוֹצִיא

הוֹרִיד \ יוֹרִיד

רָחָב מוֹרֶדֶת אֹתָם בְּעַד הַחַלּוֹן

ירד | וַיּוֹרֶד | הוֹרֵד | הוֹרִיד

---

her'á / yar'é
HI: show
Jael is showing Barak Sisera.
(Judg 4:22)

hotsí / yotsí
HI: bring out
Joshua is bringing out kings from
the cave. (Josh 10:23)

he'elá / ya'alé
HI: bring up; offer up (a sacrifice)
Joseph's brothers are bringing him
up from the cistern. (Gen 37:28)

horíd / yoríd
HI: lower, take down
Rahab is lowering them through the
window. (Josh 2:15)

5.4
Personal Pronouns

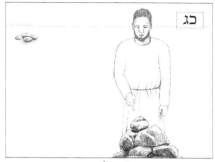

זֶה \ זֹאת

לְאָ֫רֶץ הַזֹּאת וְלַבַּ֫יִת הַזֶּה

אֵ֫לֶּה

מָה הָאֲבָנִים הָאֵ֫לֶּה לָכֶם

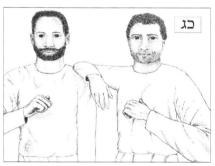

אֲנִי · אָנֹכִי

עִבְרִי אָנֹכִי וְאֶת־יְהוָה אֲנִי יָרֵא

אֲנַ֫חְנוּ

אָ֫נָה אֲנַ֫חְנוּ עֹלִים

zé / zót
PRO: this (m/f)
"... to this land and to this house."
(2 Chron 7:21)

aní / anoxí
PRO: I (c)
"I am a Hebrew, and I fear YHWH."
(Jon 1:9)

éle
PRO: these (c)
"What do these stones mean to
you?" (Josh 4:6)

anáxnu
PRO: we (c)
"Where are we going up?"
(Deut 1:28)

אַתָּה

לֹא־טוֹב הַדָּבָר אֲשֶׁר אַתָּה עֹשֶׂה

אַתֶּם

אַתֶּם עֹבְרִים אֶת־הַיַּרְדֵּן

אַתְּ

וַיֹּאמֶר בַּת־מִי אַתְּ הַגִּידִי נָא לִי

אַתֵּן · אַתֵּנָה

וְאַתֵּן צֹאנִי צֹאן מַרְעִיתִי

---

atá
PRO: you (ms)
"The thing that you are doing is not good." (Exod 18:17)

át
PRO: you (fs)
"Whose daughter are you? Please tell me." (Gen 24:23)

atém
PRO: you (mp)
"You are crossing over the Jordan." (Num 33:51)

atén / aténa
PRO: you (fp)
"And you are my flock, the flock of my pasture." (Ezek 34:31)

הוּא

וְהוּא כֹהֵן לְאֵל עֶלְיוֹן

הֵם · הֵ֫מָּה

וְהֵם לֹא יָדְעוּ כִּי שֹׁמֵעַ יוֹסֵף

הִיא

כִּי הִיא הָיְתָה אֵם כָּל־חָי

הֵ֫נָּה

וַיִּרְאוּ בְנֵי־הָאֱלֹהִים כִּי טֹבַת הֵ֫נָּה

---

hú
PRO: he; that (ms)
And he was priest to God Most
High. (Gen 14:18)

hí
PRO: she; that (fs)
... because she was mother of every
living person. (Gen 3:20)

hém / héma
PRO: they; those (mp)
And they did not know that Joseph
was listening. (Gen 42:23)

héna
PRO: they; those (fp)
And the sons of God saw that they
were good. (Gen 6:2)

5.5
Prepositions

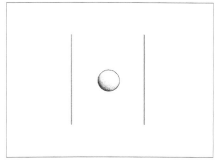

בֵּין

וַיָּשֶׂם לַפִּיד בֵּין־שְׁנֵי הַזְּנָבוֹת

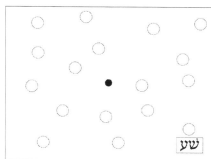

תָּוֶךְ · תּוֹךְ

וּמִפְּרִי הָעֵץ אֲשֶׁר בְּתוֹךְ־הַגָּן

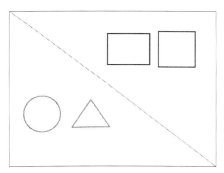

כְּ- · כְּמוֹ

כָּמוֹנִי כָמוֹךָ כְּעַמִּי כְעַמֶּךָ

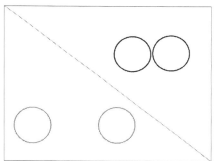

עִם · אֵת

לָמָּה תֵלֵךְ אִתָּנוּ שֵׁב עִם־הַמֶּלֶךְ

---

bén
PREP: between
And he placed a torch between the
two tails. (Judg 15:4)

kə / kəmó
PREP: as, like; according to
"I am as you, my people as your
people." (1 Kgs 22:4)

távex / tóx
N: middle, midst of
"But from the fruit of the tree in the
midst of the garden ..." (Gen 3:3)

ím / ét
PREP: with
"Why do you walk with us? Dwell
with the king!" (2 Sam 15:19)

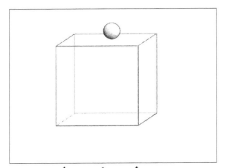

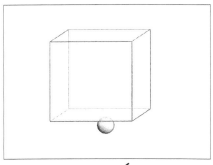

עַל · מֵעַל

וַיָּשֶׂם עַל־הַמִּזְבֵּחַ מִמַּעַל לָעֵצִים

תַּחַת

וְהוּא־עֹמֵד תַּחַת הָעֵץ

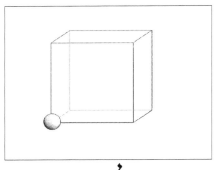

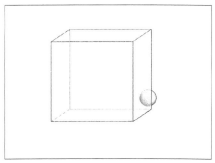

לִפְנֵי

וַאֲבָרֶכְךָ לִפְנֵי יְהוָה לִפְנֵי מוֹתִי

אַחַר · אַחֲרֵי

הִנֵּה עַבְדְּךָ יַעֲקֹב אַחֲרֵינוּ

ál / má'al
PREP: on, above; against; about
And he placed (him) on the altar on
top of the wood. (Gen 22:9)

táxat
PREP: under; instead of
And he was standing under the tree.
(Gen 18:8)

lifné
PREP: in front of, before
"And I shall bless you in front of
YHWH before I die." (Gen 27:7)

axár / axaré
PREP: behind, after
"Behold, your servant Jacob is
behind us." (Gen 32:21*)

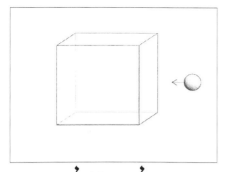

לְ- · אֶל

וַיֹּאמֶר לָהּ שׁוּבִי אֶל־גְּבִרְתֵּךְ

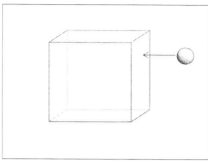

עַד

עַד־בֹּאֲכֶם עַד־הַמָּקוֹם הַזֶּה

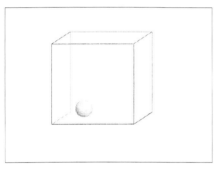

בְּ-

אָכֵן יֵשׁ יְהוָה בַּמָּקוֹם הַזֶּה

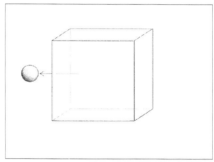

מִן

וַיִּקְרָא מַלְאַךְ יְהוָה מִן־הַשָּׁמַיִם

---

lə / él
PREP: to, toward, for
And he said to her, "Return to your
mistress!" (Gen 16:9)

bə
PREP: in, by; with; against
"Surely YHWH is in this place."
(Gen 28:16)

ád
PREP: until; while, during
"... until you came up to this place."
(Deut 1:31)

mín
PREP: from, out; than; because
And the angel of YHWH cried out
from heaven. (Gen 22:11)

5.6
Question Words

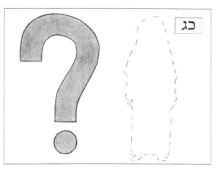

מִי   מָה

וַיֹּאמֶר לוֹ יִצְחָק אָבִיו מִי־אַתָּה   וַיִּקְרָא פַרְעֹה מַה־זֹּאת עָשִׂיתָ לִּי

why?

הֲ-   לָמָה

הֲשֹׁמֵר אָחִי אָנֹכִי   לָמָה לֹא־הִגַּדְתָּ לִּי כִּי אִשְׁתְּךָ הִיא

mí	*má*
PRO: who?	PRO: what?
And Isaac his father said to him, "Who are you?" (Gen 27:32)	Pharaoh called out, "What is this you have done to me?" (Gen 12:18)
ha	*láma*
(indicator of yes/no question)	why?
"Am I the keeper of my brother?" (Gen 4:9)	"Why did you not tell me that she is your wife?" (Gen 12:18)

5.7
English Translations

אוֹ	or	כִּי	because, that; but
אָז	ADV: then, at that time	כִּי אִם	except, but rather
אֵין	there is not	כֵּן	ADV: thus, so
אַךְ	but, only	לֹא	no, not
אַל	no, not	לְבַד	ADV: alone, besides
אִם	if	לָכֵן	therefore
אָמַר	Q: say	לְמַעַן	PREP: on account of;
אַף	even, indeed		in order that (with inf.)
אֲשֶׁר	who, that, which	מְאֹד	ADV: very
אֵת	object marker	מָלַךְ	Q: reign
בִּלְתִּי	no, not	מְעַט	ADV: little, few
בְּעַד	PREP: behind; for	מַעֲשֶׂה	N: deed, action
גָּדַל	Q: grow up, be great	מַרְאֶה	N: appearance
גַּם	ADV: also, even	נָא	please
הַ	the	נָבִיא	N: prophet
הָיָה	Q: be, become; happen	נֶגֶד	PREP: opposite, in front
הֵן	behold, look	עוֹד	ADV: again, still, yet
הִנֵּה	behold, look	עָשָׂה	Q: do, make
וְ	and; but, then	פֹּה	ADV: here
חָזַק	Q: be strong	פֶּן	lest, or else
חָיָה	Q: live, be alive	פַּעַם	N: time (occurrence)
יַחַד	ADV: together	קָדַשׁ	Q: be holy
יַחְדָּו	ADV: together	רָבָה	Q: be(come) many
יַעַן	PREP: on account of	רַע	Q: be bad, be evil
יֵשׁ	there is	רַק	ADV: only
כַּאֲשֶׁר	just as	שֶׁ	who, that, which
כֹּה	ADV: thus, here	שָׁם	ADV: there

GLOSSARY

א

אָב	father	60
אָבַד	perish	97
אֶבֶן	stone	27
אֱדוֹם	Edom	92
אָדוֹן	master	63
אָדָם	humankind	42
אֲדָמָה	ground	24
אָהַב	love	134
אֹהֶל	tent	108
אוֹ	or	155
אוֹר	light	21
אָז	then	155
אֹזֶן	ear	45
אָח	brother	61
אֶחָד	one	116
אָחוֹת	sister	61
אַחַר	after	150
אַחֵר	another	114
אֹיֵב	enemy	96
אַיִל	ram	31
אַיִן	there is not	155
אֵיפָה	ephah	111
אִישׁ	man	41

אַךְ	but	155
אָכַל	eat	49
אַל	not	155
אֶל	God	80
אֶל	toward	151
אֵלֶּה	these	145
אֶלֶף	thousand	119
אֵם	mother	60
אִם	if	155
אַמָּה	cubit	111
אָמַר	say	155
אֱמֶת	truth	66
אֲנִי	I	145
אֲנַחְנוּ	we	145
אָסַף	gather	131
אַף	nose	45
אַף	indeed	155
אֵפוֹד	ephod	54
אֶצְבַּע	finger	44
אַרְבַּע	four	117
אָרוֹן	chest	77
אַרְיֵה	lion	33
אֹרֶךְ	length	112
אֲרָם	Aram	93

אֶרֶץ	land	22
אֵשׁ	fire	25
אִשָּׁה	woman	41
אַשּׁוּר	Assyria	93
אֲשֶׁר	which	155
אַתְּ	you (fs)	146
אֵת	with	149
אֵת	object marker	155
אַתָּה	you (ms)	146
אַתֶּם	you (mp)	146
אַתֵּן	you (fp)	146

ב

בְּ	in	151
בָּא	come	123
בָּבֶל	Babylon	93
בֶּגֶד	clothing	54
בְּהֵמָה	livestock	30
בוא	(root of בָּא)	
בּוֹשׁ	be embarrassed	135
בָּחַר	choose	130
בָּטַח	trust	135
בין	(root of בֵּן)	
בֵּין	between	149
בַּיִת	house	105
בָּכָה	cry	134
בְּכוֹר	firstborn	62
בָּלַע	swallow	49
בִּלְתִּי	not	155
בָּמָה	high place	77

בָּן	understand	99
בֵּן	son	61
בָּנָה	build	107
בְּעַד	through	155
בַּעַל	owner	72
בָּקָר	cattle	30
בֹּקֶר	morning	37
בִּקֵּשׁ	seek	65
בְּרִית	covenant	86
בֵּרַךְ	bless	88
בֶּרֶךְ	knee	44
בָּשָׂר	meat	50
בַּת	daughter	61

ג

גָּאַל	redeem	59
גְּבוּל	border	91
גִּבּוֹר	warrior	96
גָּדוֹל	big	113
גָּדַל	be great	155
גּוֹי	nation	83
גָּלָה	depart	127
גִּלָּה	uncover	53
גִּלְעָד	Gilead	92
גַּם	also	155
גָּמָל	camel	32

ד

דִּבֶּר	speak	101
דּוֹר	generation	60

דֶּלֶת	door	106
דָּם	blood	78
דֶּרֶךְ	path	108
דָּרַשׁ	inquire	85
דֶּשֶׁא	grass	29

ה

הַ	the	155
הֲ	question mark	155
הֵבִיא	bring	142
הֵבִין	explain	99
הִגִּיד	tell	67
הוּא	he	147
הוֹדָה	thank	81
הוֹלִיד	beget	59
הוֹלִיךְ	lead	89
הוֹצִיא	bring out	143
הוֹרִיד	lower	143
הוֹשִׁיעַ	save	89
הֶחֱזִיק	hold tightly	140
הֵחֵל	begin	132
הִיא	she	147
הָיָה	be	155
הֵיכָל	temple	76
הִין	hin	111
הִכָּה	strike	95
הֵכִין	prepare	142
הִכְרִית	cut off	140
הָלַךְ	walk	125
הִלֵּל	praise	81

הֵם	they (m)	147
הֵמִית	kill	97
הֵן	behold	155
הֵנָּה	they (f)	147
הִנֵּה	behold	155
הֵנִיחַ	give rest	142
הֵסִיר	remove	53
הֶעֱבִיר	send across	141
הֶעֱלָה	bring up	143
הֶעֱמִיד	position	141
הִצִּיל	rescue	89
הִקְטִיר	make smoke	75
הֵקִים	raise up	141
הִקְרִיב	bring near	140
הַר	mountain	25
הֶרְאָה	show	143
הִרְבָּה	multiply	59
הָרַג	slay	95
הֵרִים	lift up	141
הֵרַע	do evil	73
הֵשִׁיב	return	142
הִשְׁלִיךְ	throw	130
הִשְׁמִיעַ	proclaim	140
הִשְׁתַּחֲוָה	bow down	81
הִתְהַלֵּךְ	walk about	109
הִתְהַלֵּל	boast	137
הִתְחַזֵּק	strengthen self	137

ו

וְ	and	155

ז

זֹאת	this (fs)	145
זֶבַח	sacrifice	75
זֶּבַח	sacrifice	74
זֶה	this (ms)	145
זָהָב	gold	27
זָכַר	remember	87
זָקֵן	elder	42
זֶּרַע	seed	51

ח

חֶדֶר	room	106
חֹדֶשׁ	month	36
חוה	(root of הִשְׁתַּחֲוָה)	
חוֹמָה	wall (city)	105
חוּץ	outside	77
חָזַק	be strong	155
חִזַּק	strengthen	138
חָטָא	sin	73
חַטָּאת	sin	72
חַי	living	79
חָיָה	live	155
חַיָּה	animal	30
חִיָּה	let live	139
חַיִל	wealth	80
חָכָם	wise	79
חַלּוֹן	window	106
חִלֵּל	profane	73
חֵמָה	wrath	66
חֲמוֹר	donkey	32

חָמֵשׁ	five	117
חֲמִשָּׁה	fifty	119
חָנָה	encamp	109
חֶסֶד	steadfast love	86
חָסֵר	be lacking	133
חֲצִי	half	112
חָצֵר	courtyard	76
חֹק	statute	84
חֻקָּה	statute	84
חֶרֶב	sword	94
חָשַׁב	think	99

ט

טַבַּעַת	ring	55
טוֹב	good	71
טָמֵא	be unclean	73
טַעַם	taste	49

י

יָד	hand	43
ידה	(root of הוֹדָה)	
יָדַע	know	99
יְהוָה	YHWH	80
יוֹם	day	37
יַֿחַד	together	155
יַיִן	wine	51
יָכֹל	be able	135
יָלַד	give birth	59
יֶֿלֶד	boy	41
יַלְדָּה	girl	41

יָם	sea	23
יָמִין	right hand	43
יָסַף	add	115
יַעַן	on account of	155
יָצָא	go out	123
יָרֵא	fear	135
יָרַד	go down	125
יַרְדֵּן	Jordan	22
יְרוּשָׁלַם	Jerusalem	91
יָרַשׁ	take possession	95
יִשְׂרָאֵל	Israel	91
יֵשׁ	there is	155
יָשַׁב	sit	124
ישע	(root of הוֹשִׁיעַ)	
יָשָׁר	straight	79

כ

כְּ	as	149
כַּאֲשֶׁר	just as	155
כָּבֵד	heavy	113
כָּבֵד	honor	139
כָּבוֹד	glory	80
כֶּבֶשׂ	sheep	31
כֹּה	thus	155
כֹּהֵן	priest	78
כון	(root of נָכוֹן)	
כֹּחַ	strength	47
כִּי	because	155
כִּי אִם	except	155
כֹּל	all	112

כָּלָה	be finished	107
כִּלָּה	finish	132
כְּלִי	vessel	55
כְּמוֹ	like	149
כֵּן	thus	155
כָּנָף	wing	33
כִּסֵּא	chair	100
כִּסָּה	cover	53
כֶּסֶף	silver	27
כַּף	palm	43
כִּפֶּר	atone	75
כָּרַת	cut	87
כָּתַב	write	101
כָּתֵף	shoulder	44

ל

לְ	to	151
לֹא	not	155
לֵב	heart	47
לְבַד	alone	155
לָבַשׁ	wear	53
לחם	(root of נִלְחַם)	
לֶחֶם	bread	50
לַיְלָה	night	37
לָכַד	seize	130
לָכֵן	therefore	155
לָמָּה	why?	153
לְמַעַן	in order that	155
לִפְנֵי	in front of	150
לָקַח	take	129

לִקְרַאת	meet	69
לָשׁוֹן	tongue	46

מ

מְאֹד	very	155
מֵאָה	hundred	119
מְגִלָּה	scroll	100
מִגְרָשׁ	pastureland	24
מִדְבָּר	desert	25
מַה	what?	153
מוֹאָב	Moab	92
מוֹעֵד	appointed place	77
מוּת	(root of מֵת)	
מִזְבֵּחַ	altar	74
מַחֲנֶה	camp	94
מַטֶּה	staff	62
מִי	who?	153
מַיִם	water	23
מָכַר	sell	115
מָלֵא	be full	133
מִלֵּא	fill	138
מַלְאָךְ	messenger	68
מְלָאכָה	occupation	86
מִלְחָמָה	battle	94
מָלַךְ	reign	155
מֶלֶךְ	king	83
מַמְלָכָה	kingdom	83
מִן	from	151
מִנְחָה	gift	74
מִסְפָּר	number	116

מְעַט	few	155
מְעִיל	coat	54
מַעַל	above	150
מַעֲשֶׂה	action	155
מָצָא	find	65
מִצְוָה	commandment	84
מִצְרַיִם	Egypt	93
מָקוֹם	location	24
מַקֵּל	stick	29
מַרְאֶה	appearance	155
מִשְׁכָּן	tabernacle	76
מִשְׁפָּחָה	family	60
מִשְׁפָּט	judgment	84
מִשְׁתֶּה	feast	50
מֵת	die	97

נ

נָא	please	155
נְאֻם	declaration	68
נִבָּא	prophesy	67
נָבִיא	prophet	155
נֶגֶב	Negev	22
נגד	(root of הִגִּיד)	
נֶגֶד	opposite	155
נָגַע	touch	132
נָהָר	river	23
נוח	(root of נָח)	
נוס	(root of נָס)	
נָח	rest	107
נַחַל	stream	23

נַחֲלָה	inheritance	62	סֵפֶר	document	100
נִחַם	relent	88	סִפֵּר	recount	67
נִחַם	comfort	139	סָר	turn aside	123
נָחָשׁ	snake	33			
נְחֹשֶׁת	bronze	27		ע	
נָטָה	stretch out	69	עָבַד	work	107
נכה	(root of הִכָּה)		עֶבֶד	slave	63
נָכוֹן	be ready	133	עֲבֹדָה	service	78
נִלְחַם	fight	95	עָבַר	pass over	126
נִמְצָא	be found	137	עֵגֶל	calf	31
נָס	flee	127	עֲגָלָה	wagon	108
נָסַע	journey	109	עַד	until	151
נַעַל	sandal	55	עֵדָה	congregation	68
נַעַר	young man	42	עוֹד	again	155
נָפַל	fall	133	עוֹלָם	forever	35
נֶפֶשׁ	soul	86	עָוֹן	transgression	72
נצל	(root of הִצִּיל)		עוֹף	bird(s)	33
נִרְאָה	appear	137	עֵז	goat	32
נָשָׂא	pick up	129	עָזַב	leave	130
נָשִׂיא	leader	63	עֲטָרָה	crown	55
נִשְׁאַר	remain	127	עַיִן	eye	45
נִשְׁבַּע	swear	67	עִיר	city	105
נָתַן	give	129	עַל	on	150
			עָלָה	go up	125
	ס		עֹלָה	burnt offering	74
סָבַב	go around	126	עַם	people	83
סָגַר	shut	131	עִם	with	149
סוּס	horse	32	עָמַד	stand	124
סוּר	(root of סָר)		עַמּוּד	pillar	76
סָפַר	count	115	עַמּוֹן	Ammon	92

עֵנָב grape....................51

עָנָה answer 65

עָפָר dust.....................25

עֵץ tree....................29

עֶצֶם bone....................47

עֶרֶב evening................37

עָשָׂה do.....................155

עָשָׂר teen.................118

עֶשֶׂר ten.....................118

עֶשְׂרִים twenty.............119

עֵת time 35

עַתָּה now....................35

פ

פֶּה mouth 45

פֹּה here...................155

פֶּן lest....................155

פָּנָה turn 126

פָּנִים face.....................46

פַּעַם occurrence 155

פָּקַד visit.....................69

פַּר bull 31

פֶּרַח flower 29

פְּרִי fruit 51

פָּתַח open..................131

פֶּתַח opening.............108

צ

צֹאן flock....................30

צָבָא army 96

צַדִּיק righteous.............71

צִוָּה command............85

צָפוֹן north 22

ק

קָבַר bury 97

קָדוֹשׁ holy 79

קָדַשׁ be holy..............155

קִדֵּשׁ consecrate........138

קָהָל assembly............68

קוֹל voice....................66

קוּם (root of קָם)

קוֹמָה height................112

קִיר wall (house).......106

קְלָל curse 88

קָם get up..................124

קָנָה buy....................115

קָרָא call out..............101

קָרַב come near 126

קֶרֶב entrails................47

ר

רָאָה see 132

רֹאשׁ head....................44

רִאשׁוֹן first 114

רַב many.................113

רָבָה become many 155

רֶגֶל foot 43

רָדַף chase................127

רוּחַ spirit 21

רוֹם	(root of רָם)		שָׁב	return	123
רוּץ	(root of רָץ)		שָׁבוּעַ	week	36
רֹחַב	width	112	שֵׁבֶט	rod	62
רֶכֶב	chariot(s)	94	שבע	(root of נִשְׁבַּע)	
רָם	be high	81	שֶׁבַע	seven	117
רָע	be evil	155	שָׁבַר	break	87
רַע	evil	71	שַׁבָּת	Sabbath	36
רֵעַ	neighbor	63	שׁוּב	(root of שָׁב)	
רָעָב	famine	50	שָׁחֵת	destroy	88
רֹעֶה	shepherd	89	שָׁכַב	lie down	124
רעע	(root of רָע)		שָׁכַח	forget	87
רָץ	run	125	שָׁכַן	dwell	109
רַק	only	155	שָׁלוֹם	peace	66
רָשָׁע	wicked	71	שָׁלוֹשׁ	three	116
			שָׁלַח	send	69
שׂ			שִׁלַּח	send away	139
שָׂדֶה	field	24	שֻׁלְחָן	table	100
שׂים	(root of שָׂם)		שְׁלִישִׁי	third	114
שָׂם	set down	129	שלך	(root of הִשְׁלִיךְ)	
שָׂמַח	be happy	134	שָׁלֵם	whole	113
שִׂמְלָה	garment	54	שִׁלַּם	(re)pay	138
שָׂנֵא	hate	134	שָׁם	there	155
שָׂפָה	lip	46	שֵׁם	name	42
שַׂר	commander	96	שָׁמַיִם	heaven	21
שָׂרַף	burn	75	שֶׁמֶן	oil	78
			שְׁמֹנֶה	eight	118
שׁ			שָׁמַע	hear	101
שֶׁ	which	155	שָׁמַר	keep	85
שָׁאַל	ask	65	שֹׁמְרוֹן	Samaria	91
שאר	(root of נִשְׁאַר)		שֶׁמֶשׁ	sun	21

ENGLISH INDEX

Made in the USA
Middletown, DE
05 September 2019